AF655646

CONTEMPORARY INDIAN ENGLISH FICTION

A Comic Vision

Dr. Trailokya Nath Parida
Dr. Itishri Sarangi

AUTHORSPRESS

Worldwide Circulation through Authorspress Global Network
First Published in 2022
by
Authorspress
Q-2A Hauz Khas Enclave, New Delhi-110 016 (India)
Phone: (0) 9818049852
E-mail: authorspressgroup@gmail.com
Website: www.authorspressbooks.com

Contemporary Indian English Fiction:
A Comic Vision
ISBN 978-93-5529-161-5

Copyright © 2022 Dr. Trailokya Nath Parida & Dr. Itishri Sarangi

All rights reserved. No part of this publication may be reproduced, stored in a retrieval system, transmitted or utilized in any form or by any means, electronic, mechanical, photocopying, recording or otherwise, without the prior permission of the authors.

Printed in India at Thomson Press (India) Limited

Preface

The faculty of laughing is a unique gift to human beings which is not bestowed at millions of other flora and fauna. The sources of human laughter are varied and numerous. The basis of humor comes out from the funny activities, oddities, shortcomings and behavioral dysfunctions of people and also frequently from desperation, violence and suffering. The literature of several nations or languages may not be complete without the genre of humor. Humor is the quality of being amusing or comic expressed in literature or speech and it is an aspect of life that helps us to stand and fight. Humor is a comic laughter or incongruous quality that causes amusement. On the other hand, satire is a very powerful artistic form with a corrective purpose of human behavior. Satire aims at rectifying different institutions in the society. The present critical study attempts to explore to explore the above two vital elements of Contemporary Indian English Fictions for the benefits of the students.

Itishri Sarangi

Acknowledgement

I am greatly indebted to my parents who have extended their enthusiastic support to fulfil my dream of preparing this book. I acknowledge my gratitude to all academic colleagues for their untiring care and continuous inspiration to write on the light moments of life. At last, I thank everyone who has been approachable indifferent to their positions in the course of my journey for my indomitable effort.

Itishri Sarangi

Contents

Preface 5

Acknowledgement 7

1. Role of Humour and Satire in Literature 11
2. The Rise of Novel in Indian English Literature 23
3. Development of Novel in Post-Independence Period 26
4. Humour and Satire in British Literature 30
5. Upamanyu Chatterjee's Novel *Mammaries of the Welfare State*: A Scathing Satire against Indian Bureaucracy 43
6. Comic and Satiric Aspects in Upamanyu Chatterjee's *English August: An Indian Story* 55
7. Comic Portrayal of Power-Hungry Politicians in Anurag Mathur's *Making the Minister Smile* 65
8. The Comic Vision in Anurag Mathur's *Inscrutable Americans* 72
9. A Satirist as the Guardian of Ideals in Anurag Mathur's *The Country is Going to the Dogs* 81
10. Humour as the Heart of Literature in Chetan Bhagat's *Half Girlfriend* 87
11. Sharp Reflection of Maladies that Afflict Indian Society at Various Levels: An Analysis of Chetan Bhagat's 2 *States: The Story of My Marriage* 99

Bibliography 122

Index 128

1

Role of Humour and Satire in Literature

Usually, writers employ their comic vision to rectify the shortfalls and errors of human beings. George Meredith's (1828-1909) *Essay on Comedy and the Uses of Comic Spirit* (1877) considers as the excellent test of the civilization of a country to be "the flourishing of comic idea and comedy" and it is of the true comedy that "it shall awaken thoughtful laughter" (Meredith 140).

Humor is the spirit of literature. It is the tendency of specific cognitive experiences to incite laughter and offer amusement. All around the world and through different point in time people retort to humor. 'Satire' is meant to be a literary art of diminishing or derogating a subject by making it ludicrous and entertainment, derision, scorn or resentment. This form of literature exposes and criticizes people's stupidity and vices in the contemporary or topical issues. Satire is a kind of literature in which vices, follies, abuses and shortcomings are held up to ridicule ideally with an intention of offending individuals, corporations, government or society into further advancement. The basic aim of satire is to bring changes in the society with positive criticism.

The study deals with the elements of humor and satire in the fictional narratives in Indian English literature published during and after nineteen-eighties with particular focus on the novels of Upamanyu Chatterjee, Anurag Mathur and Chetan Bhagat. The trio have been successful in appropriating the use of humor and satire with an intention of articulating the absurdity of traditional beliefs and superstitions of rural India. Each of them have mentioned the aspirations of the middle class to attain the life of prosperity and comfort; the neo-colonial attitude of exploitation of the poor and innocent Indians by those who appropriate power through dishonest and deceitful means. Novels of the above writers refer to the grotesque ways of imitating western life styles and manners and self-seeking mindset of politicians and bureaucrats. The elements of humor and satire in the fictional narratives take reference from selected novels of the contemporary novelists. Novel, as the form of literature very often employs humor and satire as a weapon to reach at the huge number of readers. According to Iris Murdoch (1919-1999) "Fiction must contain comedy if it attains a realistic portrayal of human life" (Hague 9). As fiction mirrors life, the literary form has been well used by some writers around the world to expound the lighter side and hideous things of our life. The purpose of comic vision is to satirize a given circumstance, which the world literature has witnessed a lot.

The history of Indian English Novel traces the development of Indian novel from its beginning in the late 19th century. In the contemporary Indian English fiction, Upamanyu Chatterjee, Anurag Mathur and Chetan Bhagat are three distinguished creative writers who use humor and satire to make light of serious and often taboo subjects; sometimes generating discomfort ,serious thoughts as well as amusement to the audience .Each of these novelists stands out for this uniqueness but all three of them have adopted common narrative techniques of employing humor and satire in decoding the complicate, multiple existences of an individual in a postmodern era. While Upamanyu Chatterjee's novels predominantly inform scathing satire against Indian bureaucracy and moral depravity, the novels of Anurag Mathur are comic portrayals of the power-hungry politicians and the pseudo elite ways of the idolizing the west. Chetan Bhagat's novels are on the other hand are a sharp reflection of the maladies that afflict Indian society at various levels of life and living in terms of the comic mode of burlesque and satire.

Humor is the heart of literature. Without humor literature is a tasteless curry without spice. David Lubar (1954), a prolific writer, famous for his humorous books remarked in an interview that just as humor fits into most areas of art and entertainment, it fits into literature "where it brings pleasure, eases pain and makes the world a better place" (www.tjprc.org > publishers > 2-40-13...). From the very beginning of British literature humor got its mark to the next generation. For instance, since Chaucer's *Canterbury Tales* in the fifteenth century, writers have been making us laugh with humorous writings. On the other hand, satire is the genre of literature in which evils in the society and individuals are held up for ridiculing them with the intention of rectifying individuals and society for improvement. When humor is always funny satire may not be always funny. The real purpose of satire is to bring a change through constructive social criticism using wit as weapon and to minimize the impeding and wider issues of the society. Both humor and satire have been used in different forms of literature but most successfully in the form of novel. British and Indian literatures have the elements of these aspects in various literary works. William Thrall, Addition Hibbard, and C. Hugh have mentioned about the meaning and function of a satirist in *A Handbook to Literature*. "The true satirist is conscious of the frailty of institutions of man's devising attempts through laughter not so much to tear them down as to inspire a remodeling" (Thrall, et al 436).

In *The Language of Humor*, Alison Ross (1949) remarks regarding the social aspect of comic elements and opines that perhaps the most important role of humor is to induce laughter. It reduces pain and lightens difficult situation. He defines humor as "something that makes a person laugh or smile" (1). Jerry Palmer in his *Taking Humor seriously* interprets humor as "everything that is actually or potentially funny, and the process by which this funniness occurs"

Novel as a literary form is a colonial child in India. The Indian English novel before independence directly deals with nationalistic feelings as central themes. On the contrary the postmodern Indian novel deals with different themes. The change in the content of the novel has necessitated the use of the new technical devices in the novel.

Most of the studies done so far in this aspect of Indian writing in English related to humor and satire confine itself to the overall view of the concepts and history of it. Different studies have glimpses on the evolution of the novel in India and its root in literature. Many researchers, educationists and professors have compiled a wide range of writings on Indian English fiction but much not done on the specific study of humor and satire in the same. The thesis aims at the thorough study on this specific genre in contemporary Indian English fiction on three selected novelists suited to the purpose.

Wit and Humour in Indian English Literature (2008) edited by Ramesh. K. Srivastav stresses on humorous elements in the contemporary Indian English novels. Srivastav's introductory remark explicates the purpose of comic elements which is mainly to provoke laughter.

In *Post Modern Indian English Fictions* (2008) Prof. Jitendra Narayan Patnaik, a writer and critic, emphasizes on the fantasy, humor and satire. "The comic mode seemed especially appropriate to articulate the irrationality of traditional beliefs and superstitions of rural India, the aspirations of the middle class to attain a life of prosperity and comfort, the neo colonial attitude of exploitation of the poor and innocent Indians by those who appropriated power through corrupt and devious means and the self-seeking mindset of politicians, bureaucrats and businessmen" (Pattnaik 34).

A close analysis in this regard shows that the three distinguished novelists namely Upamanyu Chatterjee, Anurag Mathur and Chetan Bhagat have employed humor and satire to create laughter and to attack the shortfalls of the society. Each of these novelists stands out for their uniqueness for utilizing the same in an effective way. Chatterjee is one of the important figures in the domain of Indian novel who has profound and comic vision and lasting impression on the readers. Among the contemporary writers, who have stunned the literary world with their works, Upamanyu Chatterjee is outstanding and influential and the style of writing is muscular and vibrant. The novelist's narrative strategy is sophisticated in its use of irony and farcical comedy. Chatterjee is gifted with an extraordinary talent for irony, satire and black humour in his novels.

Chatterjee always tries to depict the comic aspects of everyday life. Various forms of comedy like farce, satire and irony got reference through perfect techniques. Chatterjee's Last *Burden* (1993), *English, August* (1988), *Mammaries of the Welfare State* (2000), *Weight Loss* (2006), and *Way to Go* (2010) are clear examples of the description of the emergence of humor and satire. His *English, August: An Indian Story* (1988) is well written and interestingly funny. The stupendous and remarkable aspect of this novel is the use of humor. The story centers round a city boy Augustya, profoundly influenced by the western culture is stranded in a small village with a job in which the protagonist has no interest at all. The western culture and its impact on young generation together with visible difference between urban and rural lives are also another theme which is beautifully described. The fiction is a witty commentary on the mammoth apparatus on the Indian bureaucracy with its inefficient administrative officers. "During these years, Agastya Sen's perception of the absurdities of bureaucratic life around him becomes sharper and his irreverent attitude towards the grotesque ways in which civil servants function turns bitter and wry" (Patnaik 45).

Chatterjee's comic elements in *English August: An Indian Story* is quite impressive and heart touching. Akas Kapur observes on the protagonist o the novel and comments, "Agastya's story is convincing, entertaining, moving and timeless. It merits accolades that is far harder than to earn than authentic. It's a classic" (www.complete-review.com >august).

Anurag Mathur is an Indian author who is successful in depicting the novels with elements of humor and satire to a great and outstanding degree. Mathur's *Inscrutable Americans* (1991), *Making the Minister Smile* (1996), *The Department of Denials* (2004) and *The Country is going to the Dogs* (2014) are some successful literary creations on the context of humor and satire. Chatterjee's

Inscrutable Americans is a hilarious and poignant novel about an Indian student who had spent a year in a small American university. The fiction looks into the clash of Indian culture and an America that is both hilarious and exhilarating to a smart but naive foreigner.

Today's fictional scenario presents Chetan Bhagat as a famous Indian author who has penned down a number of novels that attract and hit the current market with huge success. Bhagat steps in the arena of the Indian literary scene with a number of novels like, *Five Point Someone* (2004), *One Night at the Call Centre* (2005), *The Three Mistakes of My Life* (2008), *2 States: The Story of My Marriage* (2009), *Revolution 2020* (2011), *What Young India Wants* (2012), *Half Girlfriend* (2014) and *One Indian Girl* (2016) which are stupendous fictional creations attracting huge number of readers. Bhagat's *Half Girlfriend* is a fictional account of life in the IIT campus. Chetan Bhagat, undoubtedly applauded as a versatile genius in relation to the issues and problems of youth and their concerns through humor and satire. The author always tries to give voices to unheard feelings, emotions, opinions and inner thought, liberty and freedom of the youth. *Half Girl Friend* is deeply rich with mentions of heart touching humor that drag a great number of followers of him. Moreover, his technique to attack the orthodox and traditional beliefs is memorable forever. His *'2 States: The Story of My life'* deals with the attack on the so-called traditional beliefs in the family. Bhagat did a fantastic job for making the readers more interesting throughout the novel. The fiction is all about family and how important it is to get the family's approval before union of two love birds. Usually couples not only in India but also in the world enjoy very much. Among the prominent writers, Chetan Bhagat is an imperishable name in the arena of postmodern fiction. In fact, it is true that Bhagat has tried his hands in present-day writing and has been successful in reigning over hearts of millions of readers. No other writer has managed to reach out such an extensive range as Bhagat who writes for the masses. Bhagat's originality in content makes the readers feel that it is their story. The narrative strategies of humor and satire are really suitable. The novels are a sharp reflection of the maladies that afflict Indian society at various levels of life and living in terms of the comic mode of burlesque and satire. Apart from dealing with harsh realities of life, Bhagat's fictions manage to maintain the sense of pure humor with well-defined and interesting plot. Complications and conflicts are evidently observable to keep the readers entertained. Bhagat tries to appeal the general public and most of Bhagat's novels

This is an attempt to provide a conceptual idea of humor and satire and its role in literature. This chapter provides a bird's eye view on the theory of humor and satire and offers to have a reference to the elements of humor and satire in British and Indian English fiction. This section of the study is a glimpse into the various findings of humor and satire in two different literatures concerning to the wide sociological and moral issues of the society. This book explores the manifestations of laughter and criticism through forms of humor and satire. Besides there will be a comprehensive study on the origin of humor and satire, with various implications. Role of each distinctive element of humor and satire is to be studied that evokes different kinds of fun and sense of pleasure among the audience.

The book examines the appropriateness in using humor and scathing satire in the works of Upamanyu Chatterjee against Indian bureaucracy and moral depravity. Chatterjee's novels are fabulously intelligent, amusing and especially curious about modern India. Most of Chatterjee's novels are also the portrayals of so called Indian middle class and are manifestations of deviations from normal conditions that seem as tough and problematic. Chatterjee's preoccupation, playfulness, sarcasm, humor and irony are prevalent in most of the novels. Although the corpus of Chatterjee is not vast, the bulk is a powerful emergent voice in Indian post-colonial literature. Chatterjee's novels are having striking aspects with incredible language that touch the common masses in the society which makes the readers oscillate between the beauty of high serious prose and the ridiculous emotions that the fiction covers. *Last Burden* and *English August* are the striking examples. His writings are glaringly amusing and instructive denting at the irrational attitudes of bureaucracy and the higher society. This chapter contains introduction on the novelist and hints the comic sense and intention of rectifying the society.

Again, it explores the comic and satiric elements in the works of Anurag Mathur. The novels of Anurag Mathur are chiefly known for his comic portrayals of the power-hungry politicians and the pseudo elite ways of idolizing the west. The study makes an assessment of Anurag Mathur as a novelist who is full of laughter, wit and surprises with a subtle tinge of social satire. Mathur's novels take a close look at the corruption rampant in the political circles with a sardonic sense of humor. Mathur writes of India that is so funny and sinister. Fictional world of Mathur abounds with recognizably demented characters. Perhaps each of these novels is a mirror of incongruous sell as he starts out on the road to a globalized society. Among all his works *Inscrutable Americans* comes to the category of perfect humorous fiction with a hilarious story concentrating on the mishaps and adventures of a village Indian in the USA.A number of true observations take humorous reference.

An assessment is made of Chetan Bhagat as a novelist and the subtle use of humor and satire to bring about the stark reality of life. Bhagat's novels are the manifestations of sharp reflection of the maladies afflicting Indian society at various levels of life and living in terms of comic mode of burlesque and satire. Presently another genre of the fictional writing is gaining momentum is the campus or academic novel. Campus or academy is a place that attracts most people because of its impawning idealistic notions. The inmates dedicate themselves to their lofty pursuits. The novels narrate tales of dreams and disappointments, intrigues and manipulations, love and longing, friendship and enmity, curiosity and casualness, career and concerns and job worries in the lives and activities of the educational institutions. In fact, Bhagat is one of the leading novelists of this school of fiction writing in India. The current chapter is a comprehensive study of findings of use of humor and satire by the novelist to reach at the huge numbers of readers. The first section is a brief introduction on the writer and the rest is a close study of the text of two novels to extradite the references of humor and satire at different stages of his works. As it is a herculean task to include all novels, the study covers only two major novels with their themes in brevity.

It is unquestionably impossible to cite all the findings and coverage of all the major issues and examples, trends and theories but it is an honest attempt to justify the comic and satiric elements of the mentioned writers in an appropriate approach. Findings on the rapid changes of Indian novels in the context of different issues like independence, struggle and miseries of human beings that took a diversion with the clash between faith and realism, between tradition and modernity and searching for individual identity are the point of discussion.

There is a possibility of further study on the impact of world literature on the modern-day Indian English literature. Apart from this, researchers can explore the combination of native humor and satire as a driving force for destabilizing and transforming the power structure of the colonizer. Noted Indian author, Jitendra Narayan Pattnaik has written several books on contemporary Indian English fiction. In *Post Modern Indian English Fictions,* Pattnaik writes on the aspects of humor and satire in contemporary Indian English fiction. He traces the Indianness in the process of creating humor and satire, the core of current literature. Hence there is a possibility of further study in Indian English literature related to it. Again, philosophical dimension of contemporary literature is subject to further study. Adolescence and youth centered approach of these contemporary fiction writers in creating humor and satire leads to further study by the researchers. Adolescence is a subject matter in various forms of literary practices in different stages of literary history. Even during the Middle Ages prior to the invention of printing press adolescence did exist in the texts like *Beewolf* in the west and much earlier like *The Ramayana* and *The Mahabharat.* But it is also a significant issue to explore whether the adolescence literature has attained its due status in today's fictions among the contemporary writers. Apart from this how contemporary youth is caught between cultures is another aspect of further study. Hence researchers in coming days can attempt these aspects for their supplementary study.

Literature mirrors the society. Humor and satire are two important elements of literature. Both humor and satire fulfill the objectives of literature. They are closely related. Humor is meant to make people laugh where satire is used to attack the vices or follies of the society or individuals. Humor is one of the crucial aspects of everyday life and the tool that we can use to face our hardest times that we confront in different situations. Even some critics opine that humor is the key to get happiness and to reach at the climax of success in society. Not only the individual himself gets happiness but also others become participants of this aspect. Humor brings laughter with positive emotions which simply keep us in a better mood and makes everyone around us happier. Moreover this element of literature lightens the mood and resolves many critical problems. We can change our life doomed with dark shadows with humor and positive emotions. Without humor life seems harder to handle. This might be the cure to a miserable life that goes through hardship and struggling.

Literature is considered as a reflection of good values and lacks in the society. The purpose of the writers is to bring desired changes in a constructive way. Satire is a technique used by the writers to expose and criticize foolishness and corruption of an individual or a society by the use of humor, irony, exaggeration or ridicule. It targets to get better humanity by criticizing. The writer mocks at something that he doesn't like. One of the techniques that satire uses is irony. Irony focuses on the discrepancies between what is said and what is meant.

The thought of how humors soothe us is not new which is just a tonic is for us in our burdened life. Humor is rightly said to be the best medicine. Michael (1941) also concerns with this, "Laughter is a therapy. It is healing. As a tonic for what ails us…if we hurt, we laugh. And laughing we heal" (1-2). The fictional narratives in Indian English, during and after nineteen eighties have employed humor and satire appropriately and to a remarkable extent which necessitate attention among the researchers. Novelists like, Upamanyu Chatterjee, Anurag Mathur and Chetan Bhagat are quite impressive in respect of using these elements in literature.

They articulate the foolishness of established beliefs and superstitions of rural India. The aspirations of the middle class to grip prosperity in life and the attitude of dysfunctional bureaucrats to exploit the poor and innocent Indians provide them wide areas to make a number of light moments in their novels and attack the vices and follies in the society. Both British and Indian literature employ humor and satire to such a great extent that is difficult to avoid.

Humor is defined as "the quality of being amusing or comic and the ability to make other people laugh especially as expressed in literature" (Keenoy, 112). Humor is the heart of literature. Without humor, literature is tasteless curry with no spice. G.K.Chesterton (1874-1936), one of the prolific critics, rightly says "Literature is leisure but humor is necessity" (21). In fact, humor and satire are the distinct elements of literature. We use humor and satire differently with diverse purposes. Humor means the quality of being funny, which is the propensity of specific cognitive experiences to incite laughter and provide amusement. People from all around the globe pay attention to humor with great interest. David Lubar (1954) rightly remarked in an interview, "Just as humor fits into most areas of art and entertainment it fits into literature that brings pleasure softens tired minds and makes the world a better place". Humor is often used in literature. It is not a genre but a substance of literature. Humor concerns with emotional aspects. Concerning social aspects of the term, Ross (1998) defines "something that makes a person laugh or smile" (1). Palmer (1994) provides a more sophisticated definition and says humor is "everything that is actually or potentially funny, and the process by which this funniness occurs" (3). Beginning from the Chaucer's age writers have been making us laugh with humorous writing through a long time. It is one of the most effective literary weapons to please the audience. It helps the readers to get interest, sustains their concentration, helps them to get united with the characters, emphasizes and connects thoughts and helps the readers to picture the situation. It also provides surprise and revelation.

The word 'satire' comes from the Latin word '*satura*'. *The Oxford English Dictionary* indicates the term that dates back to the 16th century and some other critics opine that it originates from the

Latin word '*satira*', later form of '*satura*', meaning medley. *The Oxford Companion to English Literature* defines satire as a poem or prose composition in which "prevailing vices or follies are held up to ridicule". However, in the *Current Literary Terms: A Concise Dictionary*, Arthur Scott defines satire as "The holding of vices or folly to ridicule. It makes use of irony and sarcasm" (257).

M.D. Fletcher, a prolific critic and renowned writer who has delivered several critical books on satire, calls it, "verbal aggression in which some aspects of historical reality is exposed to ridicule" (ix) "Satire can be defined as the literary art of diminishing or derogating a subject by making it ridiculous and evoking towards it attitudes of amusement, contempt scorn, or indignation." (Abrahams. M.H & Geoffrey Galt Harpham (352). In addition to it, Frank Palmeri, Professor of English at the University of Miami states, "Satiric narrative works indirectly through parodic alteration of celebratory forms, established discourses, and dogmatic pronouncements" (1). A great Canadian commentator Rex Murphy points out that "we throw the term 'satire' around rather too generously these days and it's a free upgrade when making simple fun of someone passes as satire" (9).

Oxford Advanced Dictionary defines 'satire', "The use of humor, irony, exaggeration or ridicule to expose and criticize people's stupidity or vices particularly in the context of politics and other topical issues". Satire intends to reform and rectify institutions and persons and aims to clear folly, anguish and evil. Again, it targets at criticizing individuals, corporations, government or society itself to perfection. Although satire is used to be comic, its greater principle is to have a beneficial 'social criticism' using wit to draw attention to both particular and broad issues in civilization. On the other hand, a satirist aims to bring changes by creating a situation for the individuals to feel ashamed on the basis of his follies and mistakes. Satirists practise it as a corrective of human mistakes. "Satire has usually been justified, by those who practice it as a corrective of human voice and folly" (Abrams 352).

2

The Rise of Novel in Indian English Literature

There are different forms of writings developed in Indian English Literature like poetry, prose and drama, but interestingly fiction as a possible literary form through which a writer can hope to keep himself in constant touch with the common readers. Usually, writers get themselves established through this genre. The bulk of Indian English Literature is in the novel form. In fact, the growth of the novel in the later years achieved success compared to other forms of literature, Fiction was in fact last to turn up in the literary scenario of Indian English literature. Fiction as the most influential and dominating form of literary expressions today has attained an impressive image in Indian English literature. Fiction is the most appropriate literary form for the examination of experiences and thoughts in the framework of our time. In fact, Indian English novel has its depth not only India but also in the world. Prof. M.K. Naik rightly remarks, "[...] one of the most notable gifts of English education to India is prose fiction for though India was probably a fountain head of storytelling, the novel as we know today was an important from the west". Today's fiction differs in its context and content leading to a substantial degree. Margaret Hillenbrand (1972) comments, "Today novels are considered to be entirely concerned with the social or economic or psychological forces that they by necessity exhibit, or with those details of daily life that are for the good novelists only to some deeper end" (Hillenbrand 61).

However Indian writers in English have contributed appreciably to this specific field of novel. Novel as a form of literature appeared as a popular form during the eighteenth-century England. Gradual democratization in Great Britain leads to a rapid development of novel. But the novel is a new to India and gained the ground gradually. K.R. Srinivas Iyengar says, "For the novel, properly so called have to wait till the latter half of the eighteenth century" (2).

The novel emerges as one of the most forceful and convincing literary genre recent years. It has been widely accepted as the appropriate form for the searching of new experiences and thoughts in today's world. "The 'novel' as a literary phenomenon is a new to India. Epics, lyrics, dramas, short stories and fables have their respectable ancestries, going back by several centuries, but it is only a period little more than a century that the novel – the long-sustained piece of prose fiction – has occurred and taken root in India. (Iyengar 314) "Although the 1930s are generally seen as the take-off decade for the Indian novel in English we can trace its genealogy quite far back into the previous century" (Mehrotra 105). Indian English fiction has acquired extensive commendation, distinction and prestigious position in recent times in the whole world. The history of novel in India is aligned to the advent of the Britishers in India spanning over more than two hundred years. Such a prolonged and momentous reign by Britishers had its adverse as well as beneficial effects in the nation. Leaving out their ruthless colonization; The Britishers did leave their impact in their literary, architectural and political sides. However, the western influence had a great impact on the Indian English fiction. The early Indian English novel is derivative and imitative of English models. Early novelists imitated the works of English Romantics and Victorians. However, the literary and artistic sides perhaps had overshadowed all the other existences.

Novel as a form of literature emerges out of peculiar social circumstances and deals with human predicaments in its nature. Indian novel in English gained a great momentum gradually but outstandingly after the publication of Bankim Ch Chatterjee's (1838-1894) *Rajmohan's Wife* in 1864. In connection of nationalism in Chatterjee's novel, Makarand.R. Paranjape comments, "Indeed it is not at all unusual to read Bankim as one of the creators of the Indian nationalism [...]" (163).

Indian English novel has gone to the next range considerably in volume, variety and ripeness. Novel, the small plant at the initial stage, has now accomplished a copious expansion and branched off in a variety of dimensions. The Indian English novel has begun its journey through the eruption of scorching and blistering talks of Henry Derozio, the religious prose of Tagore and the peace-loving dictums preached by the great nationalist Mahatma Gandhi. The birth of Indian English novel in India is to some extent, the result of historical, political, social and cultural incidents. Mainly Indian struggle for independence, Gandhian Movements and the partition of India are the raw materials for the birth and growth of the English novel. Dr. Gajendra Kumar says, "The first half of the twentieth century has been rich and fruitful period for the Indo – Anglian novels which show the profound influence of the epoch making political, social and ideological changes because of the Gandhian Movement" (5). As an iconic figure Gandhi had a drastic satiric attitude towards industrial system of production. The two factors, namely the independence movement and nationalistic spirit and its combination paved the way for much momentum and stimulate to the outpouring of novels in India. Love and fondness for the native land was the driving force which acted as patriotic sentiments of the masses for further momentum. Although early Indian fictions are the depiction of patriotic spirits even, we can find deviation to it. For example: Nirad. C. Chaudhuri (1897) viewed India contrary to previous objectives. Chaudhury discarded the fiery *Kandan's* patriotism and spiritualism. The themes of Indian novels revolved round the influential spirits of struggle for independence. Raja Rao's *Kanthapura* (1938), K.S.Venkatramani's *The Patriot* (1934) and Mulkraj Anand's *Untouchable* (1935), *Coolie* (1936), *The Sword and The Sickle* (1942) are fittest examples. The Indian English was a ripe fruit that tested and digested by the world readers with the success of Rabindra Nath Tagore bagging Nobel Prize for literature.

3

Development of Novel in Post-Independence Period

Literary works produced after independence, have presented many faces of Indian culture and tradition and search for the greater values in the society. In searching the best form of literature fictions grounded its foot prints better but gradually. Novels written in post-Independence period retained the momentum that had achieved during the Gandhian age. The tradition of social realism established earlier, made its appearance now. Novelists like Bhabhani Bhattacharya (1906-1988), Manohar Malgonkar (1913-2010) and Kushwant Singh (1915-2014) are noted figures during the nineteen fifties and the early sixties.

The trio in the history of Indian English literature namely, Mulk Raj Anand, Raja Rao and R.K.Narayan were the novelists who stabilized and fortified the Indian English fiction with their abundance of literary outputs and their distinctive literary style. Their appearance was the most outstanding event in the dominion of Indian English fiction. R.S. Singh mentions, "The purpose of fiction was clear; to rouse the masses and instill in them a sense of responsibility and dedication either to the land of a glorious past or to the one that had fallen on evil days. The reformist zeal was predominant and the political plight a major obsession" (Singh 44).

They are the true exponents of the Indo-English novel. Walsh said, "It is these three writers who defined the area in which the Indian novel as to operate. They established its assumptions; they sketched its main themes, freed the first models of its characters and elaborated its particular logic. Each of them used an easy, natural idiom which was unaffected by the opacity of a British inheritance. Their language has been freed of the foggy taste of Britain and transferred to wholly new setting of brutal heat and brilliant light (62).

Indian English fiction achieved a recognizable status for the literary works of Mulk Raj Anand who has been most important among others. He writes with personal commitment. Anand's contribution to the Indian English fiction of social realism is undoubtedly enormous and unsurpassable. Anand's *Untouchable* (1935) portrays the story of a boy from the low caste. His *Coolie* (1936) depicts protagonists affected by sheer poverty. He was having sympathy for the poor and downtrodden. Both of these fictions are supplication for oppressed, the underprivileged and the outcast, who face economic adversity and emotional embarrassment in an unbending social arrangement. At his initial writing he preferred to write the familiar to the fancied.

R.K.Narayan (1906-200) is one of the most popular literary figures in Indian English literature along with rest of the 'Big Three'. Narayan is the most prolific Indian novelist in English from a south Indian middle-class family and is the first to portray a purely Indian sensibility. According to K.S.Srinivas Iyengar "He is one of the few writers in India who take their craft seriously, constantly striving to improve the instrument, pursuing with a sense of dedication what may often seem to be the mirage of technical perfection. There is a norm of excellence below which Narayan cannot possibly lower himself." (Iyengar 359). He remained unapproachable towards the modern-day socio, political issues and explored the south Indian middle class setting in his fiction. Narayan's works include *Swami and Friends*, (1935), *The Bachelor of Arts* (1937), *The Dark Room* (1938), and *The English Teacher* (1946). R. K.Narayan's fictional arts got maturity only after independence. His next stage of writing includes *The Financial Expert* (1952), *The Guide* (1958), and *Man Eater of Malgudi* (1962).

Raja Rao (1908-2006) is a renowned writer in Indian English Literature and the youngest of the great trios. Rao's arrival on the literary scene has been described as the emergence of a new star in this area. Rao's area of literary outputs includes *Kanthapura* (1938*), The serpent and the Rope* (1960), *The Cat and the Shakespeare* (1965), *Comrade Kirillov* (1976) and *The Chess Master and His Moves* (1988) are important. Rao's *Cat and the Shakespeare* is a metaphysical comedy. The creative genius of these 'big trios' examines minutely the Indian sensibility and expose the Indian way of life which makes their works quite attractive. M.K.Naik rightly remarks, "Reverence and irreverence, fantasy and reality, mysticism and mammonism, the past with its age old philosophy and the present of the global war-are all mixed together in thus brief teasing fable" (179).

After the independence of India Indian English literature had many ups and downs with tough challenges to face and many changes came over Indian way of existence. Different political, social and cultural issues led the Indian writers to be independent with self-confidence and broadened vision. Consequently, developments and important gains were registered. The convention of social realism flourished to a great extent which was initiated by Mulk Raj Anand.

After 1960s, however Indian English fiction took a new direction with a shifting from public to private. To some extent it followed western concept of writing. The mass destruction and the turbulence over the world brought unrest and anxiety. As literature mirrors the society, the novelists cannot remain aloof from the current trend. Hence Indian novelists are not exclusion to the recent changes and developments. Outstanding literary figures like Anita Desai, Arun Joshi and Nayantara Sahgal changed the face of Indian English novel through their works that contain seeds of the future expansion of Indian English fiction.

The postmodern Indian English novel emerged decisively with Salman Rushdie's literary creations. Anita Desai observes Rushdie as "the voice of a new age" (Anita Desai vii). Although Rushdie was a religious controversial writer, the volume of satiric reference didn't stop. In connection to this Rod Mengham observes Rushdie's writing as, "Secular authorship verses religious fatwa, profit against Prophet...such sound bites and headlines are the stuff of Rushdie Affair" (183).

The contemporary Indian English Fiction has created its own niche in the twenty first century Indian English literature. It has become, in recent years, one of the most dynamic areas of the literary pursuit in India. This is the new generation of the novelists that include many pioneering novelists who have great impressions on the huge number of readers and have shaped the Indian reading habits. This group of writers include writers like Anita Desai (1937), Despande (1938), Salman Rushdie (1947), Manju Kapur (1948), Amitav Ghosh (1956), Kiran Desai (1971), Arundhati Roy, Gita Hariharan (1954), Sobha De (1948), Sashi Tharoor (1956), Upamanyu Chatterjee (1959), Anurag Mathur and Chetan Bhagat (1974).

4

Humour and Satire in British Literature

Although Chaucer (1343-1400) is primarily known for his love poems and his *The Canterbury Tales* (1387-1400) brilliantly portray the attitudes and traditions of the medieval period. There is an attack on the areas of love, marriage and religion in a comic and satiric way. The Prologue to *The Canterbury Tales* gets appreciation for the energetic and vigorous individualized portraits. These aspects claim to be the indicative of social humor and satire. Humour began in British literature with the story telling tradition of Chaucer. The development of the story telling tradition along with ironies paved the way resulting from the concurrence of people from different classes and opinions. Carter Roland (1942) rightly comments, "This theme of joy and pain of love becomes more and more important through Chaucer's writing". (30). Since *The Prologue* initiates with humor and satire. The book begins with the Knight who is described as being perfect and brave. Apart from this, Chaucer begins to dig at the Knight. Chaucer thinks to be an ideal warrior but at the same time believes to be very mild which shows a humorous contrast. Albert Edward (1951-2006) rightly remarks, "Success in descriptive passage depends on vivacity and skill in presentation as well as on judgment shown in the selection of details. Chaucer's best descriptions of men, manners, and places are the first rank in their beauty, impressiveness and humor" (37). Humor can be social corrective and forms unity and consistency bringing together a group with common principles to take pleasure in a form of play or joke. *The Wife of Bath*'s *Prologue and Tale* has a kind of humor. Albert writes, "In literature of his time, when so few poets seem to have a perception of the fun in life, the humor of Chaucer is invigorating and delightful. The humor, which steeps nearly all his poetry, has great variety: kindly and patronizing, as in the case of the clerk of Oxford; broad and semi facial as in the *Wife of Bath*; pointedly satirical as in the *Pardoner and the Summoner...*" (37-38) On Chaucer's characters Bhim. S. Dahiya writes, "Chaucer's treatment of his characters reveals the power structure of the social hierarchy of his day" (12).

As a greatest myriad minded personality and an ever-popular dramatist, William Shakespeare's works are extraordinarily outstanding and noteworthy for the use of humor and satire. In fact, there is quite a bit of humor in Shakespearean comedies. Shakespeare uses light hearted tone with happy ending. In his comedies much of fun arises from the misconception of lovers. His *Much Ado about Nothing* (1600), *As you Like it* (1623) are quite amusing and entertaining. Afterwards Shakespeare's comedies are quite impressive for the vernacular and street humor. Again, Shakespeare's festive humor in his romance, histories and dark humor in tragedies are really wonderful.

The eighteenth century is the golden age of satire and aims at rectifying the society through criticizing its members and ridiculing established standards of thoughts. It tries to bring Great Britain's flaws and discipline the double standards of the time. This is the period in which exaltation of wit and rationale come to the front of literature in the form of both Horatian and Juvenalian satires. Different mediums of satires are in use by the great masters of this area like Alexander Pope (1688-1744) and Jonathan Swift (1667-1745). On Swift, Dr. Raghukul Tilak comments, "Swift is the prince of English satirist. In his satires he lashes with rare zeal at all kind of aberrations and departures from the normal" (275). Again, David Daiches writes about Swift's typicality as, "Swift's misanthropy was of peculiar kind" (608).

They use different types of reason and target to scorn in order to stand out as a separate aspect of British society. In *Rape of the Lock* Alexander Pope skillfully chide society in a refined voice to criticize the follies and false ego of the greater classes. "Pope had in common with Dryden, considerable success in translating Greek and Latin classics especially Homer –into English and also prepared a note, if flawed, edition of Shakespeare, in 1725" (C. Roland and J. McRAE 142). During Restoration Congreve established the comedy of manners. Congreve's *Love for Love* (1695) and *The Way of the World* (1700) focus on social class and social hypocrisy.

Humor or laughter occupies a large place in the Victorian literature. Humorous references are visible in most of literary creations in this era. Among them the great novelists like Charles Dickens (1812-1870) and William Makepeace Thackeray (1811-1863) deserve a warm discussion. "It is very likely that that the reputation of Dickens will be maintained chiefly as humorist. His humor is broad, humane and creative. It gives such real immortals as Mr. Pickwick, Mrs. Gamp, Mr. Micawber, and Sam Weller-typical literary brotherhood" (Albert 392). The life of Charles Dickens can be seen to reflect the scholarly patterns of the late eighteenth century. "The vein of good-natured comedy, well observed character, humorous use of class and dialect difference, and 'traditional values will be found repeatedly in Dicken's works." (Carter Ronald and John McRAE, (251) Again Dicken's hum our goes deep and his satire appears amazing to later generation. "Dicken's humor is not very subtle, but it goes deep and in expression it is free and vivacious. His satire is apt to develop into burlesque..." (Albert 392). W. Boegoe wrote, "Dickens is still read for his fun..." (187) Dicken's *Hard times* is a superb example of satire against the society he lived. "Hard Times is actually one of the less rich and rewarding of Dicken's novels, but in many ways his most accessible critique of the society he lived in" (253). Disappointment and disillusionment dominate in Dicken's *Great Expectation. "Great Expectation* marks the change from David Copperfield. Here the hero bears a close-up semblance to Dickens himself ... (ibid). Satire serves as an instrument of socio-political protest. Moreover, it acts as a reinforcement of class, imperialist, and antifeminist ideologies.

M.K.Naik (1942), in *A History of Indian English Literature* remarks, "Indian English Literature began as an interesting by-product of an encounter in late 18th century between a vigorous and enterprising Britain and a stagnant and chaotic India" (01). Indian English literature is an independent body of work of writers writing in English whose native and co-native language could be one of the several languages of India. They are Indian by birth, ancestry or nationality. The phrase Indo-Anglian is used to describe the original creative writing by the Indians. According to K.R.S. Iyengar (1908-1999), there are three types of Indian writings in English, first those who have acquired their entire education in English schools and universities. Secondly Indians who have settled abroad but are constantly in touch with the changing surrounding and the traditions of their country of adaptation and finally Indians who have acquired English as a second language. On the concept of Britisher's attitude that suited to the colonized Indians for the language Ketaki Datta writes, "Contrary to the popular belief the foreign masters never encouraged their native subjects to use English as a medium of self-expressions [...] This attitude suited to the colonized Indians very well" (xi).

It is the outcome of many factors like British rule in India, English education, acceptance of English as an official language, impact of western thought and culture. All these influences and many more brought about a revolutionary change in Indian English literature. The factors that shaped, molded and helped the Indian English literature arose much from the political and social problems of a colonized country. The Indian English Literature is comparatively new source. It is only one and half century old. In fact, the first book written in Indian English was *'Travels of Dean Mohomet'* which is a travel narrative by Sake Dean Mohomet and was published in England in 1793. At the initial stage western literature had a great impact on Indian Literature particularly in the area of novel. However, most of the early Indian writings in English were in non-fictional work. Most of them were based on biographies and political essays.

Humour and Satire in the Indian English Fiction

Humor and satire got effectiveness among the contemporary Indian English novelists successfully. They intend to articulate the irrationality of traditional beliefs and superstitions of rural India. They referred to the aspirations of the middle class to attain life of prosperity, comfort and the neo-colonial attitude of exploitation of the poor and innocent Indians by those who appropriate power through corrupt and devious means. They also cover the area of grotesque ways of imitating life style, manners and self-seeking mindset of politicians, bureaucrats and businessman.

Amitav Ghosh's debut novel *The Circle of Reason* (1986) starts with a note of humorous description of an eight-year-old orphan boy Alu who is adopted by his elderly uncle a teacher in a small Indian village. He arrives in Lalpukur, a village in Bengal, and startles the villagers with the strange shape of his head, "an extraordinary head-huge, several times too large for an eight-year-old and curiosity even, bulging all over with knots and bumps" (Pattnaik 3). One of the elderly villagers, Bolai-da describes the head as "alu, a potato, a huge, freshy dug, lumpy potato" (4). The novel centers around Alu who remains to be the rest of the life. Balaram, Alu's uncle practices phrenology and is obsessed with the hygienic property of carbolic acid, concludes through his strange ways of measuring different parts of the human body with a pair of calipers. Balaram's erratic behavior leads to some strange consequences. Unfortunately, Alu is involved in a local feud resulting the bombing of his home. Alu, the only survivor and the suspect in the bombing flee closely followed by young Indian police, arrives at the small Arabian state of al-Ghazira where he works as a laborer. The second part of the novel is replete with a magic realism. Once Alu is found under the collapse of a shopping mall, miraculously saved and "just a hair away from his nose" (240) After a lot of problems Alu returns to India. The plot of the novel opens with Balaram's obsessions with reason and proceeds to suggest that much of what happens is accidental, unpredictable and absurd making it a comic one.

Kiran Desai's first novel *Hullabaloo in the Guava Orchard (1998)* is a triumph in a comic story telling. The Telegraph comments as "uproarious, whimsical, and occasionally stinging. "It is the story of Sampath Chawla who escapes of the boredom of middle class living in the sleepy, North Indian town of Shahkot into the comical freedom of life on a guava tree and who mysteriously disappears along with a band of langur monkeys when the guava orchard is invaded by the army and government agencies to get rid of the monkeys.

Even contrary to the critics there are some women writers in Indian English who have made their presence through humorous writing. For instance, Namita Gokhale (1956), Suniti Namjoshi (1941) and Arundhati Roy (1961), have left an unsurpassable position in Indian English fiction. They have taken the themes such as adultery, inequities in social and legal status, lesbianism, sexual relationships, class and caste barriers as well as political satire. These three writers have explored the potential of laughter boldly. Nam Joshi's *The Conversation of Cow* is the most light hearted. Although the fiction resembles in its theme to other novels it ends in a joyous tone. The story doesn't have death at all. Nam Joshi challenges the static form of the fable. The issues like gender inequality and female subject hood are treated with parody, irony and wit. In *Paro Dreams of Passion* Gokhale has chosen a playful title that ironies the goddess, Parvati and the heroin of the legendary story who is a clinched epitome of all things virtuous and unattainable. While the erotic and economic are uneasily intertwined to provide for many hilarious situations, the anger at the gender role prescription and the marginalization of women is humorously grounded through satire. Again, Arundhati Roy's *God of Small Things* is the most satirical of the novels.

Sashi Tharoor is one of the prominent writers among the post modernists who tries to his best to satirize with different narrative strategies such as satire, pun, parody and humor. Tharoor's *Great Indian Novel* is well known for his satiric mode predominant in the novel. Tharoor has taken as existing work the Mahabharata with a serious purpose and has contextualized it with the present political condition.

The elements of humor and satire in the fictional narratives in Indian English fiction got appropriated by the three important novelists of the contemporary writers namely, Upamanyu Chatterjee, Anurag Mathur and Chetan Bhagat. The trio has been successful in appropriating the use of humor and satire with an intention of articulating the absurdity of long-established thinking and superstitions of rustic India. The aspirations of the middle class to accomplish the life of affluence and comfort, the neo-colonial attitude of exploitation of the poor and innocent Indians by those who appropriate power through dishonest and deceitful way got reference. Again, the ugly ways of imitating western life styles and behavior and self-seeking mindset of politicians, bureaucrats and businessman are satisfactorily described.

The contemporary fiction writers concentrate on the minute and the subtle aspects of human behavior and have tried to bring out multiple shades of their experiences. In an essay entitled "*Defence of the Novel*," Salman Rushdie announces the emergence of a new form the novel, a de-centered, transitional, inter-lingual, cross-cultural novel" (8). "Rushdie's implied assumption that the post-colonial novel is the quintessence of the contemporary fiction is perhaps the most appropriate way of defining the postmodern India English Fiction" (Patnaik 01).

The post-independence Indian English fiction grapples with the psychological, sociological and moral implications of transition from the colonial to the post-colonial condition. The novel embodies a decisive moment of post-colonial condition which has surmounted the agony of negotiating with colonial legacy and celebrates the hybridism as an essential and defining trait of Indian reality. Helen Tiffin remarks the post-colonial, "has been used to describe writing and reading practices grounded in some for colonial experience" (170). The post modernism encompasses radical attitudinal changes in the wake of globalization, consumerist culture and traditional perspectives and reality. "The postmodern Indian English is therefore a ramification of post-colonial discourse in its contemporary state of assimilating pluralities and multiplicities by dismantling the western binary construction of the east west as well as interrogating which is framed by meta-narratives" (Patnaik 02). The themes of contemporary Indian English novel is now centered around rural, suburban, lower and middle class lives, and thus Malgudi, Nathan, the Untouchable, Gandhism and Munoo are now important in this aspects. The new generation of novelists who are mostly born in and after nineteen-fifties, have been brought up in metropolitan and urban ethos, educated in elitist schools and colleges and their sensibilities have been nurtured by corporate and global value orientations. Therefore, it is the social reality they perceive is one of the upper classes, urban, cosmopolitan, materialistic and mercenary culture. Contemporary Indian novelists are almost uniformly united in terms of their class composition. "The social realism that the contemporary Indian English novelists use in their novels constitutes the world of bureaucracy, business, politics and cinema. Nayantara Sahgal puts it, "mix of cultures and influences of Hinduism, Islam and Christianity, of east and west" (Critical Spectrum 35)

Humour and Satire in Post-colonial Indian English Literature

People, all around the globe feel comfortable with humor and all most all cultures of the civilization respond to humor. Indian literature in English can't lag behind which takes conception during British period and started flowering afterwards. English literature has attained a great maturity with an impressive image in world literature especially over last decades. The last thirty years witnesses a great change in last thirty years. Aftermath of 1980s Indian English writing achieved new ideas and voices enriched with expression of humor and satire especially in the field of fiction. There are many novelists like, Salman Rushdie, Vikram Seth, Amitav Ghosh, Arundhati Roy, Kiran Desai, Chetan Bhagat and many more who explored many possibilities of life and literature.

R.K Narayan is another celebrity author and the founding pillar of Indian English writing enjoys a matchless position in the packed fictional scene of Indian fiction especially for the influential skill of humor and satire. Narayan's humor from different angles is remarkable. The entire story of *The Bachelor of Arts* is full of humor. Chandran's designs to see Malathi at close quarters are as humorous as the vehement quarrel of the fathers of Chandran and Malathi over the superiority of the horoscopes as if the whole world depends on horoscopes alone. The hero leaves his home because he was disappointed in love and then comes back quietly marries another girl and the transformation is as convincing as it is full of ironic laughter. Margaya's career in *The Financial Expert* is replete with a rich texture ironic humor. Boisterous carefree laughter also rings through the pages of Narayan. Swami, the schoolboy and his friends go through all sorts of funny adventures and remind us of a subdued Tom Sawyer and his gang. *The English Teacher* (1945) with its somber atmosphere has moments of laughter when Narayan describes the hostel life scenes. Mr. Sampath and Raju keep us laughing in our sleeves as they go through their career, bluffing their customers or clients, helping friends, cheating others – and ending in a complete collapse of themselves. *The Guide* (1958) shows comic moments when the villagers are shown an anti-malaria film at the fasting place of Raju, a screen-size close up of the mosquito came on the screen and the villagers declared that it was natural that with such mosquitoes, foreign people were bound to fall sick. In all his novels, intellectual idea and humor go hand in hand; his novels are pensive comedies. The key note of Narayan's concern is the minute observation and fine ironic harmonious way of telling story. Swami's cricket eleven in search of a regular or even an irregular playground is a masterpiece of narration that is equally humorous. The very creation of the character of Mr. Sampath is full of subtle irony. "The early novels with their energetic young men (Swami, Chandra and Krishna), the middle novels with the restless drifters (Srinivas, Sriram) and the later novels, with the men wounded and exiled by the modern world (Jagan, Raman) map out an emotional and intellectual journey that many middle class people in formerly colonial societies have made: the faint consciousness of individuality and nationality through colonial education; confused anti-colonial assertion; post-colonial sense of inequality and failure; unfulfilled private lives; distrust of modernity and individual assertion; and finally in middle or old age, the search for cultural authenticity and renewal in a neglected , once great past"(Mehrotra 233-234).

Shashi Tharoor is the prominent writer in the arena of postmodern Indian writings in English and gets wide impression for his experimental writing using sharp satire to attack socio, economic and political issues both in fiction and non-fictional works. Basically, an international civil servant and a star journalist, Tharoor creates image as a political thinker and an intellectual both nationally and internationally. The author achieves acclamation for his exemplary work as an International Civil Servant and also for literary career. Most significantly, Tharoor's writings are about Indian, but of universal significance. Tharoor's first novel, *The Great Indian Novel* (1989), adopts different narrative strategies like satire, joke, burlesques, sarcasm, humor and wit. The skill of using satire and parody is in fact outstanding. Tharoor has become a beacon of satirical mode in Indian Writing in English by adopting satire, an eighteenth-century literary mode, to narrate a twentieth century reality. Indian Writing in English has not given much serious attention to satire, like in English literature. Only a few writers have tried to employ satire in their writings. A.K. Ramanujan also employed satire in his poems but not as a serious mode. Shashi Tharoor made use of satire as a dominant mode in his unique way of narration. Through his writings he tries to pose more questions than giving answers, what is usually done by satirists?

To uncover the works of Salman Rushdie and his works, Mehrotra writes "Rushdie displays remarkable consistency when it comes to certain ideas, certain literary and philosophical pre-occupation and the formal means through which to achieve them. Fortunately, or perhaps unfortunately, for his readers, he is an enormously self-conscious writer whose novels, comments, and analyses in interviews and essays insistently direct attention to these pre-occupations and to his craft. Rushdie is also very erotic writer; his work is peppered with all sorts of literary echoes, allusions, and puns, each self-consciously deployed with back patting zeal and pleasure which he invites the savvy reader to share with him" (350).

Prof. Pattnaik comments, "The overwhelming reception of Salman Rushdie's Midnight's Children in nineteen- eighties led to a prolific production of fiction by Indian writers in the post Rushdie period, many of which were informed by the narrative strategies of fantasy, humor, satire and magic realism. The comic mode seemed especially appropriate to articulate the irrationality of traditional beliefs and superstitions of rural India, the aspirations of the middle class to attain a life of prosperity and comfort, the neocolonial attitude of the exploitation of the poor and innocent Indians by those who appropriated power through corrupt and devious means and the self-seeking mindset of politicians, bureaucrats and businessmen" (34).

Arundhati Roy is the best-known representative of the contemporary Indian English writers. She deserves a place in the history of English language and literature for expressing boldly: She believes in to be a writer for the victims of the modernity. She satirizes the indifferent attitudes of the government and the policy holders towards goodness of common man. *The God of Small Things,* the winner of 1998's Booker Prize Award is a true masterpiece in the realm of novels. Roy variously criticizes the caste system, the British Raj, communism, development and globalization.

Amitav Ghosh's fictional and non-fictional narratives tend to be transitional in sweep, moving restlessly across countries, continents and oceans. Ghosh's first novel, *The Circle of Reason* (1986) is typical in the sense. *The Circle of the Reason* begins with the humorous description of an eight-year-old orphan boy who arrives in Lalpukur, a village in Bengal, and startles the villagers with the strange shape of his head, 'an extraordinary head-huge, several times too large for an eight-year-old and curiously uneven, bulging g all over with knots and bumps' (Patnaik 34).

"Kiran Desai's first novel, *Hullabaloo in the Guava Orchard* (1998), which is 'uproarious, whimsical and occasionally stirring,' as the Telegraph commented and which, as The Pioneer commented, 'is a triumph in comic storytelling' (Patnaik 38). "Hullabaloo in the Guava Orchard is the story of Sampath Chawala who escapes from the boredom of middle class living in the sleepy, North Indian town of Shahkot into the comical freedom of life on a guava tree and who mysteriously disappears along with a band of langur monkeys when the guava orchard is invaded by the army and government agencies to get rid of the monkeys" (ibid).

The present thesis primarily aims at focusing the elements of humor and satire in the selected novelists namely, Upamanyu Chatterjee, Anurag Mathur and Chetan Bhagat. As the postmodern Indian English fiction attained maturity and image in the world literature by these writers my next chapters will elaborate their use of humor and satire taking selected novels of each. Hence before going to details of these writers, it is better to give a brief introduction on these three novelists in a paragraph.

Upamanyu Chatterjee is one of the most compelling new voices in the domain of the Indian novel in the English Literature that has a profound comic vision in his writing. Chatterjee is always attracted towards the comic aspects of everyday life. He uses the various forms of comedy like farce, black humor, satire and irony to portray the follies and foibles of Indian society. He is a great artisan of humor. "Upamanyu Chatterjee's *The Mammaries of the Welfare State* (2000), which won the Central Sahitya Academy award in 2004, is both a hilarious comedy and a sharp satire on the functioning of the so – called welfare state which is India" (Patnaik 45). Anurag Mathur's *The Inscrutable Americans* is a hilarious tale of the adventurous of Gopal, a twenty years old bumpkin and son of hair oil merchant in Madhya Pradesh, during the one year he spends as a student of chemical engineering in Evers vile, a small university campus in America. (Pattnaik 49). Chetan Bhagat is a revolutionary wave in current literature producing a number of humorous creations. Bhagat's *Half Girlfriend* and *2 States: The Story of my Marriage* are taken into account. Writers involve in presenting the contemporary life and living in their works. Jesse Matz writes in A Modern Novel; a Short Introduction, "The novel has been modern always concerned mainly with contemporary life, and as the name suggests, always after the new thing" (1).

Novelists around the world have contributed to the arena of fiction writing through their comic and satiric elements to touch the hearts of the readers and fulfill the objectives of literature. Since the writings of Chaucer, the literary figures have left influential impression on the audience. Chaucer developed the story telling convention along with ironies that resulted from the twist of fate of people of different classes and points of observation. Shakespeare later developed colloquial speech and street humor in his comedies, festive humor in his in his romances and histories and dark humor in his tragedies. During Restoration Congreve established the comedy of manners. The eighteenth century's satiric writings are unsurpassable. Although humorous writings are short in supply writings of the above writers is unavoidable. Indian English Literature has attained an independent status in the realm of world literature. Indian writers usually cover a wide range of themes. Among all other forms of literature novel has acquired prominent place .M.K.Naik rightly remarks, "One of the most notable gifts of English education to India is prose fiction for though India was probably a fountain head of story-telling, the novel as we know today was an importation from the west. "Generally Indian novelist's substantial contribution to the world literature is due to creative literary works generated by their novels. Among the writers in present literature Upamanyu Chatterjee, Anurag Mathur and Chetan Bhagat are most talented and quite impressive to the readers. Very few writers have managed to reach out to such wide audiences who have been a phenomenon that has affected everybody and touched everybody's life.

5

Upamanyu Chatterjee's Novel *Mammaries of the Welfare State* : A Scathing Satire against Indian Bureaucracy

Indian fiction in English witnessed a new age group of writers who provided new idea of writing through the observations of the vices and follies rampant in the society. Among the writers who brought a change in tone, tenor and content, Upamanyu Chatterjee is outstanding and powerful novelist. Chatterjee was born in 1959 and joined Indian Administrative service in 1983.The literary world of Upamanyu Chatterjee includes some beautiful creations like, *English, August: An Indian Story* (1988), *The Last Burden* (1993), *The Mammaries of the Welfare State* (2000), *Weight Loss* (2006) and *Way to Go* (2010). The investigation selects two of Chatterjee's novels i.e. *Mammaries of the Welfare State* and *English, August: An Indian Story* in order to find out elements of humor and satire.

M. David Raju writes in an article that "Chatterjee is gifted with an extraordinary talent for irony, satire and black humor. His young modern educated characters express the sense of ennui as they are restless, disinterested, unnerving, feel alienated and face the inner conflict and arduously try to find their place in the world" (Raju 195).

Upamanyu Chatterjee Chatterjee's *The Mammaries of the Welfare State* won the Central Sahitya Academy award in 2004.The present fiction enjoys worldwide acclamation from the readers. The book is amazingly brilliant and humorous. Prof Jitendra Narayan Pattnaik in *Post Modern Indian English Fiction* (2012), remarks that the novel is a comic one and provides a lot of ease moments for the readers. According to Prof. Pattnaik the novel, "(...) is both hilarious comedy and sharp satire on the functioning of the so-called welfare state, which is India" (45). *The Mammaries of the Welfare State (2000)* is a fitting sequel to his debut novel, *English August*. The novel is about the welfare state. The welfare of the people is managed by a political dynasty and civil servants. The fiction describes the protagonist Agastya Sen who is in the first year in the Indian Administrative Service. Agastya has become a veteran civil servant of the welfare state as *The Mammaries of the Welfare State* picks up some seven or eight years after the time of *English, August: An Indian Story (1988)*. Prof. Pattnaik gives an assessment on the character of Agastya and observes that "(...) during these years, Agastya Sen's perception of the absurdities of bureaucratic life around him becomes sharper and his irreverent attitude towards the grotesque ways in which civil servants function turns bitter and wry" (45). Writer and critics, Geeta Doctor in *Literature Alive,* appreciates the novel of Upamanyu Chatterjee for "the accumulation of details that produce a powerful image of Madna and the oppression of a way of functioning that passes for life in an IAS" (9).

The *Mammaries of the Welfare State* recounts the story of Agastya who is in dismay with his service. Agastya has not found happiness in the bureaucratic functions. The book finely delineates the grotesquery of governance and worthless of the administrative posts in India. Akram Mahammad writes, "The boon of civil servants becomes bane in the twentieth century India" (Vol-1, Issue 5 May 2014).

Mini Kapoor observes that the fiction is "an urbanite young civil servant's acclimatization year in hot dusty and depressing Madna" (Kapoor 30). The opening passage of the novel indicates the amount of desperation and disinterestedness as "Agastya was so enervated by his lie in the city that ever so often, when he was alone. He found himself shutting his eyes and weeping silently" (Chatterjee 3). Murari Prasad observes Agastya as, "[...] detects the bureaucratic setup, dominated hierarchy and statistics, and seeks cravings [...]. The novel is particularly harsh on the self-seeking politicians and a various bureaucrat who feed on the drugs of the Welfare State" (Prasad 12). The pangs, agony and the pressure that reigns over the administrative officer is a topic of criticism. The novelist makes an attempt to mention the various departments of the government like public health, heritage labour, culture, housing problems, police and misappropriation of public funds. Again, Chatterjee wants to make the readers aware the pervasiveness of the evils in all the walks of our life. The novel is about the journey of single Agastya, who doesn't mind smoking and submitting to the sexual advances of a forty something detached socialite greatly influenced by yoga and veganism Moreover the book is eye catching amidst an entertainingly confusing background of housing problems, transfers, goons and girls. Agastya constantly confronts the absurdities of the bureaucratic life around him.

Prof. Jitendra Narayan Pattnaik writes in his *Post Modern Indian English Fiction* that the novel "[...] is a story of Agastya, a civil servant, who confronts life and society in its myriad dimensions and is amused at the senselessness and frivolity with which a nation that claims to be welfare state conducts itself in the spheres of bureaucracy, politics and sexual relationship" (Pattnaik 48).

The story starts with Agastya in confronting himself with a housing problem. Life in the city is not good. Agastya manages to get assigned a room in The Raj Atithi Guest House, a fourteen-storey building crawling with low life in which a five-foot high wall "[...] separated its compound from the world's largest garbage dump" (5). The novelist satirizes the true picture of urbanity with bureaucratic negligence and mentions:

> The wall stretched four rows of the barbed wire, from various points of which sagged torn polythene bags of diverse colors. These contained human shit in different stages of decomposition. They'd been flung, of course, at the dump and hadn't made it across the wall. They in fact looked pathetic, like POWs in a Hollywood movie ensnared in a vain attempt to escape from a concentration camp (6).

Agastya is deeply shocked over the situation there. "Hmmm...breathe deep, my dear, this fragrant, invigorating air,' said Agastya to himself as he crossed the covered car park towards the stairs" (6). Amongst and in the twenty odd white ambassador cars there nested the low life with its charpoys, kerosene stoves, lines of washing and racing children. All sections of people are dwelling with a lot of housing problems as Chatterjee mentions as "...a million of other servants of the Welfare State in the city: he faced a housing problem" (6). Pattnaik writes on the housing problems of Agastya who is shocked "... to find himself sharing the room and its toilet with six strangers, four men and two women" (Pattnaik 46).

Satiric elements prevail here with the description of the actual condition of the Raj Atithi Guest House.

> On the first floor, Reception was a noisy ceiling fan, a declaimed-topped counter with an abandoned dinner thali on it, a flickering tube light, a vacant arm chair, and behind it on the floor a snoring maid in a blue sari. Agastya rapped on the counter, and 'koi hai?' he hollered in his we're-the-steel-frame-that's-kept-the country together voice" (6). From his room on the twelfth floor Agastya finds "a spectacular view of both the garbage dump and the slum (7).

Day to day life is frustrating for Agastya showing his discontent in different intervals. The administrational dysfunctions were horrifying. The Welfare State is a mystery within and without and getting things done is pretty much last on the list of everyone's priorities.

A good sense of ironic humor is pertinent by the novelist when Agastya finds his unoccupied second bed in his room was filled in the midst of night when was asleep. "The room had two separate beds. The second bed had been unoccupied when he'd nodded off, thinking of Daya's blue thighs and regrettably-smirking. He awoke early and abruptly to discover two men in the second bed and two women and a third man on the floor, all asleep" (7). In spite of housing problem Agastya was insecure to ask his senior about the difficulty. Usually, the bureaucratic supremacy is subject to be satirized here. "Once in the secretariat, insecure, disoriented and unhappy wanted to meet the Housing Secretary to discuss his housing problem. He couldn't because the Housing Secretary was too senior. He'd joined the civil service before Agastya had been fathered" (7). Agastya was advised to meet Menon, the Deputy Secretary who was found unpleasant to him. The way the situation is described aroused fun among the readers. "His PA told Agastya to go and call on Menon, the Deputy Secretary (Personnel Housing) instead. Menon wasn't in his room; Agastya could finally meet him two days later. Eight years ago, they had been posted together in the district of Madna and had pleasantly disliked each other" (8). Prof. Pattnaik takes into account that Agastya faces a lot of problems regarding and "[...] finds that, despite his position, it took three years before he could allot himself his own flat, he loses all hope of being allotted a flat" (46).

Again, the way the letter was written for substandard houses of type- A is quite funny.

"Subject: Invitations for Applications for Unclassified Substandard Houses of Type-A." (9). With his posting on night duty in the Secretariat Control Room, Agastya solves his housing problems partly by quietly moving into his office room and partly "by spending three to four nights a week at Daya's where he had crazy grueling sex" (35) and where he befriends Rajani, Suroor a political heavyweight. The housing problem is finally solved when Agastya is appointed Collector for Madna "to fight the plague on a war footing" (41) At least Agastya finds some female company to keep; he becomes involved with Daya, who runs the soft sell Ad agency. When Daya offers a position, Agastya remains unaffected and shows his devotion to the bureaucracy.

Again, the letter by Lina Natesan Thomas, Junior Administrator in the Ministry of Heritage, Upbringing and Resources, to the Secretary of the Welfare State was comic and satiric. The conducts unbecoming of the civil servants are quite visible expressions in a satiric mode. She finds difficulties to meet the secretary but the principal private secretary made it problematic for the inability to understand the language except Punjabi and says that he is unable to "[...] speak any other language. In fact, in your office, one gets the impressions that Punjabi is the official language of the Welfare State." (48) How the lady civil servants face uncomfortable situation in their work place is effectively satirized.

> It will not put of place to mention here that when I first arrived in this Department, in lieu of my own desk and office room, I was offered a seat on a cane sofa in the chambers of the then Deputy Secretary, Shri O.P. Chadha. I had that time complained in writing that it was neither possible nor proper for a junior administrator (Under Training), a lady officer, to function out of the chambers of the Deputy Secretary (Administration), a satyr. My complaint, which can be perused at Annexure L, had inter alia noted that Shri Chadha had verbally proposed to me that time that if I did not care for the cane sofa, I could work sitting on his lap. (Chatterjee 49).

Chatterjee presents the filthy pictures of inner and outer lives of the bureaucrats. Vijay Nambisan in *The Hindu* writes about his interview with Chatterjee regarding the present fiction in which Chatterjee admits that the novel is an admirable corrective to its prequel. There are so many people who ought Agastya Sen to be the sweet, lovable character. The protagonist is nothing of the sort who is a morally loose man in a morally loose world. Actually, Agastya is a helpless person, helpless before the huge judgment of official corruption. Chatterjee's fictional world is the offspring of his own experiences based on reality. Reality we all know is bitter experiences of life. Life is very often the jumble of the bitter and hideous experiences and he wants to present them before his readers without changing the essence, raw and uncooked. Satire is his effective weapon.

Agastya manages to escape from Madna to France pretending to do his duties. Agastya got remarks on "over the years your countries record, its performance at the Institute has been abysmal" (96). Agastya, in spite of doing something he does nothing to improve the bureaucratic conditions of the country. Again, Agastya finds himself to survive is job because of his balancing adjustment to the situation. The Welfare State on the other hand makes life complicated. Other complication includes his love life.

Chatterjee satirizes the rich, greedy, and corrupted politicians at frequent intervals. Chatterjee introduces Bhanwar Virbhim, a senior politician who served as a member of legislative assembly and has been in different positions in the government, plays caste card posing him as Don of masses. 'I am the voice of downtrodden; I am the soul of all depressed, backward, repressed, suppressed and unrecognized castes" (104). Bhanwar's son, Makhmal Bagai, a gun, notorious with his frightening temper moves around the city, abducts and molests girls in his moving vehicle and murders the victims like his father if situation demands. "...over the years the outrageous of Makhmal's offences against society and the law had kept pace with his father's increasing clout" (105). As a person Makhmal is incompetent and dangerous but his father made him to join in politics. Makhmal adopts all evil means to capture votes during election that distributes cheap whisky and beats the rival party men. Mathur criticizes the way he adopts the evil means to come to this position and remarks, "His father had wanted him to learn some of the facts of life, to revere wealth, not to remain forever retarded to grasp that money was infinitely more powerful than the gun, that nothing was socially more respectable than power, that to be on the right side of the law, one simply needed to be above it" (286).

R.P Singh rightly observes: "The Welfare State, here, doesn't mean a state for the welfare of the people but a hunting ground for predatory sharks who masquerade as public servants." The style of the fiction is sometimes serious and sometimes non-serious and very often mock serious. "We can never Eradicate Poverty...but we can eradicate the poor. All we need is intelligent legislation" (120). The fiction is a sharp, probing and penetrating pinch that gets heightened by the perfect use of mock serious tone. The fiction is full of satirical attitudes which are both cynical and realistic.

Chatterjee's keen and sharp satire is visible in a journalistic manner when it comes to official matters, presenting the true scenario of the exploitative Welfare State, "To help you to use your time more efficiently in office and to ensure that you are economical in the use of the stationery and property of the Welfare State, your kind attention is drawn once more to rule 17c (iv) of section 28 of chapter 111.I quote and verbatim from the revised Manual. Please note that the Manual was last revised not in the last century, but in 1981...The last procedure, observed too often in our offices, smacks of laziness and lack of discipline. Also, its end products reflect rather badly the financial resources of the Welfare State" (124). Through the protagonist Chatterjee attacks the mindset of the bureaucrats regarding non-attention of the grass root problems of the society. When there was a problem locally, the civil servants bring another bigger crisis to minimize the former one. Plague had affected Madna, a hinterland town which was a big problem. At this crucial juncture, Priminister was about to visit to see his hospitalized friend making the visit more important. "...the crisis, by Welfare State standards, just wasn't critical enough. When faced with a crisis, what all civil servants longed for was a bigger crisis. In the bureaucratic mind, the tensions of the demonstration, for example, were easily resolved by an outbreak of the plague, which in turn could be totally wiped out by the worst calamity of all, the visit of Priminister" (163).

Chatterjee attacks the indifferent attitudes of the government officials towards the poor and the deprived section of the society. The novel is more interesting that most of them intend to fulfill their personal aspirations instead of the welfare of the people. Dr. Onorary Kansal, the chairman of the commission misuses the state government helicopter to bring his sleeping suit from his home without having empathy to the rest. At the same time Agastya witnessed the cases of poverty that had compelled people to be bonded labor even for seventy-five rupees for year. "The bounty of welfare extends in all direction and knows no bounds; only the niggardly and the short-sighted think of economics. In a large country you have to think big" (283).

R.P.Singh rightly comments, "...The Mammaries of the Welfare State has its theme the day to day regimen of the corrupt and depraved mandarins of the welfare state. People like the high state official Bhupen, Raghupati, the politician Makhamal Bagal. The astrologer Baba Mastaram, the artist Rajani Suroor and several others play out the daily drama of venality and depravity on the bare bosom of the Welfare State" (Singh 51). Chatterjee ridicules the nepotism adopted by the political dynasty 'Aflatoon'.

Murari Prasad writes "Agastya detests the bureaucratic setup, dominated by hierarchy and statistics and seeks cravings...The novel is particularly harsh on the self-seeking politicians and avaricious bureaucrats who feed on the dugs of the Welfare State. "The novelist gives a glimpse on how the politicians and the bureaucrats are dysfunctional contrary to the notion of the Welfare State. The novel is full of innumerable instances of humor that turns sometimes into black humor which Chatterjee is gifted with. Chatterjee's rare talent of wit, satire and black humor is concerned with the official absurdities of the Welfare State. Raghupati, the chief Revenue Divisional commissioner at Madna and who served in different positions at center was an icon of proud vicious and corrupt civil servants with excessive greed for power and position is highly criticized by the novelist. Raghupati manipulates things to his own desire and utterly misused his position and commits a ghastly sin in his pooja room which indicates that his religious belief, meditation and faith in God is less important to his physical desire. R.P.Singh comments, carnal desire is "...a running motif at the level of fantasy as well as physically, and forms a crucial component of the exploitative psyche of the mandarin-politician nexus." (32). Again, the writer satirizes the nonfunctional attitudes and emptiness of the administrative functionaries. Agastya feels that the Welfare State is overloaded with many employees and officers of no importance. Moreover, Chatterjee ridicules the various schemes, loans and projects which are misused by the beneficiaries as well as the sanctioning authorities.

Chatterjee attacks the existing politicians of the welfare state and compares them as inferior to the highly experienced and even retired bureaucrats when he mentions that the senior most civil servants are "…at the end of their careers have worked at all kinds of Government jobs for thirty-five years on the job Training, absolutely, and probably more effectively than Plato's more formal, academic cultivation of body and mind" (429).

The Protagonist as an Alienated Youth

Chatterjee's novels are basically realistic in its approach and bear the testimony of an Indian novelist's sheer power to hold its readers in its strong grip. Though Chatterjee's literary works are pure world of entertainment, the novels go through lively, simple, lucid but powerful language. Chattaerjee is capable of amusing his readers with wave of new skills to entertain them. Most of his protagonists are mainly youth of emerging modern India. They represent a disdainful youth, adolescence and successive growth. The internal colonization after the Britishers make feel the central character Agastya feel alienated from the society and confronts a question in himself about the rationale of existing. Sanjay Kumar rightly observes that the central character, Agastya, "suffers from inexorable sense of exile and this feeling of exile is produced in him by an acute awareness of his colonial legacy, the two mutually opposed traditions he has been a heir to" (Kumar 102). The entire plot of the novel *Mammaries of the Welfare State* vividly represents the socio-economic conditions of Indian citizen in some backwater hinterland. The fiction is the clear representation of the stark realities of India and the Indians, their typical lifestyles, of politicians, bureaucrats, businessmen, working class people and work culture in different walks of life. The fiction represents the generation of the youth deviated from the disciplined life. Again, the Indian educated youth is under the whims of intoxication and abusive drugs. The protagonist confronts the clash between the oriental and occidental waves. The lethargic life style of Indian educated youth being detached from their inner conscience is a clear indicative of the alienated youth from the main stream. The novel delightfully narrates the typical Indian psyche and ideological issues as evident in the society. Again, it is humorous, gleeful, and lightweight raillery on the Indian social ethos, social institutions and politics.

The protagonist is a prototype of large number of Indian youths from urban area. Although he is an educated youth his tendency of nonexistence to the good morals is clearly visible in the very first appearance of the novel. Existential dilemma made Agastya to develop a sense of ironic vision frequently at different occasions in the fiction. He gets fun out of boredom and indulges in mean thoughts, desires leading to pleasure from others suffering. A.K. Sing observes that, "it is more out of bewilderment and confusion that Agastya acts in the manner most unsuitable to him" (Sing 92). The novel is full of glaring satires which are really heart touching and memorable with lot of morals to the readers. Chatterjee attacks the attitudes of the bureaucrats for their carelessness towards government fund. Their excessive greed for foreign trip at the expense of public funds is perfectly criticized. When they enter administration of the center they talk much about UNICEF, ILO, IMF,FAO and plan to move around the world, "...by Jove, the wide world at one's feet, and in one's pocket-and a salary in dollars US to be spent in Kuala Lumpur, Bangkok, Geneva, New York and Paris".

Anjana Sharma, a noted critic on contemporary literature remarks in *The Hindu*, "Mammries is not for the fait hearted, for those who like their real and fictional worlds disinfected and deodorized" (www.complete-review.com >msotws). Though a bit recurring, it is a novel which demands and keeps one's interest not only by its irony asides and insides jokes but also it dares to voice a moral outrage that very rarely finds its way into fiction, especially recent Indian English fiction. *The Mammaries of the Welfare State* is a criticism of corruption, clout, caste and complacency nature that plagues the society and its values which is rampant in Indian political and administrative set up which malign the nation or the so-called welfare state.

Soumya Bhattacharya writes in *Hindustan Times*, "The Mammaries o the Welfare State has a greater breath, a broader sweep, a far bigger mélange of unforgettable characters and often dark, brooding, even scary. The humour is sometimes all black. Nonetheless it is undoubtedly funny" (www.complete-review.com > msotws). Nirmal Sandhu writes in *The Sunday Tribune* "It is hilarious satire. But the issue it focuses on is too serious to be laughed off. It provokes one to realize, how worthless one's upbringing has been when it comes to facing one's own country" (www.complete-review.com >msotws).

After all Chatterjee's satire is sharp delineated and his lingering over a range of political sagas and descriptions of the vain attempts at getting anything done are pleasurable. His story is attached with all parts of the welfare state. The character ranges from non-acting and lethargic bureaucrats, politicians and businessman. There is frustration but humors throughout the fiction and his novels are basically realistic in approach. Though Chatterjee's novels don't have much publicity hype, his writings are pure world entertainment with characters deviated from disciplined life.

6

Comic and Satiric Aspects in Upamanyu Chatterjee's *English August: An Indian Story*

The English Literature in India that spanned over the last thirty years has undergone a dramatic change which witnessed new thoughts and voices in alteration in Indian English writing. Novelists like Salman Rushdie, Vikram Seth, Amitav Ghosh, Geeta Mehta, Kiran Desai, Vikram Chandra, Chetan Bhagat and a number of other novelists explored the new possibilities of life and literature. Similarly, Upamanyu Chatterjee, one of the convincing new voices in the realm of the Indian novel in English literature who has captured a wide range of reputation for his profound comic vision in his writing. Upamanyu Chatterjee was born on 19th December 1959 in Patna, Bihar. He received his education from St. Xavier School and St. Stephen's College in New Delhi. While studying in high school, Chatterjee wrote a play which was not published at that time, but won the school drama competition. Chatterjee joined Indian administrative service in 1983 from Maharastra Cadre. Chatterjee is a published author and best known for his novel *English August: An Indian Story* which was also adapted into an acclaimed film of the same title. "Most novel progress, but this one simply chronicles an ongoing anomie and spiritual restlessness (Washington Post). Dr Nema Nidhi writes on the author in an article that Chatterjee is, "… endowed with a unique style of wry playfulness mixed with keen observation. He defies conventions and is rarely calm or normal in his novels" (Nidhi 40).

Akash Kapoor in his article "*Up in Smoke'* published in New York Review Book opines, "Upamanyu Chatterjee' English

August…, the story of a young civil servant posted to a fictional rural town was hailed as the country's Cather in the Rye – a novel …when India was uncertainly emerging from decades of economic isolation and ill-conceived socialism…" (326)

The world of Upamanyu Chatterjee, another powerful novelist of postcolonial India paints colorful world of post-independent youth in a realistic way. Chatterjee's novels are basically realist in approach and bear the testimony of an Indian novelist's sheer power to hold its readers in grip. Chatterjee's handful of short stories of which "*The assassination of Indira Gandhi*" and '*Watching Them*' are particularly noteworthy. Iris Murdoh rightly remarks that "Fiction must contain comedy if it attempts a realistic portrayal of human life," (Hague 9) In fact it is true that literature of any age is incomplete without the genre of comedy. They try to expose the lighter side of the sarcastic and hideous things in our life. The humorists also intend to attack the shortfalls of the people, society and human errors through their comic vision. Comedy as a literary form has been used by many noted writers throughout the world. On the importance of humor in life W.H Davies remarkably wrote in his famous poem, "Leisure"

> "No time to wait till her mouth can
> Enrich that smile her eyes began?' (Leisure)

George Meridith in *Essay on Comedy* (1877) Considers an excellent test of civilization of a country to be the "the flourishing of the comic idea and comedy"; and that of the true comedy is that "it shall awaken thoughtful laughter" (140). Thus, the purpose of the comic vision is to satirize he shortfalls and promote change by doing so in a comic way.

Meenakshi Mukherjee in her article 'English August an Indian Story', comments, every aspect of being an IAS trainee has been intelligently probed by the author. Chatterjee takes us inside the mind of a bureaucrat, and tries to show that they are no extraordinary beings, but very much vulnerable to all kinds of human follies.

Anjana Sharma equates Upamanyu's vision with W.B. Yeats. She writes, "Eighty years apart, culture, civilizations, even craft and temperament apart, Yeats and Chatterjee share an identical vision of a decent red, denatured world"(https://www.rjelal.com >...). *English August* is a novel, first published in 1988 and was adapted into a film of the same name in 1994. It is really a funny novel. Akash Kapur rightly remarks in The New York Times "His book displays a world rarely seen in modern Indian writing, revealing a detailed knowledge of the heartland that can result only from personal experience. English August wears the crown of the authenticity uneasily partly because the book is so charming unassuming, so natural and assured, that it would be uncomfortable with any crown at all. English August has worn remarkably well" (www.nytimes.com >books > review > up...). Agastya's story is convincing, entertaining moving and timeless. It merits an accolade that is far harder to earn than authentic. The book is a classic. On Upamanyu Chatterjee Michel Dirda writes "Upamanyu Chatterjee's affectionate yet unsparing slacker view of modern India. Most novels progress, but this one simply chronicles an ongoing anomie and spiritual restlessness. Chatterjee though excels in his description of Indian life..." (www.wasingtonpost.com > 2006/04/20).

The fiction is a story of young civil servant Agastya Sen, who joins Indian administrative service, which the author himself joined the same age in 1983.This newly appointed civil servant is sent off for one year's training in district administration in a small town named Madna. But the course of events is full of fun and satire which is heart touching. At the very outset of the novel Chatterjee aims to make the situation light. Dhrubo asks Agastya for the eight times in one hour that when to meet again as they have to depart for their posting place. Marijuana had caused acute lethargy in them. Agastya was not in position to answer. Dhrubo took the day's forty third cigarette for his lips and took a long time to find out the match box to light his cigarette. "Uh'...said Agastya and paused, for the same reason. Dhrubo put the day's forty-third cigarette to his lips and seemed to take very long to find his matchbox. His languorous attempts to light a match became frenzied before he succeeded." (01)

Agastya joins in a small district town at Madna. Again Dhrubo remarks Agastya that he is going to get into deep trouble in Madna. Chatterje's language is comic oriented and aims to ease the readers. "Dhrubo exalted richly and out the window, and said 'I've a feeling, August, you are going to get hazar fucked in Madna." (01) In fact Chatterjee is always attracted towards comic aspects of everyday life and uses various forms of comedy like farce, black humour, satire and irony to portray the follies and foibles of Indian society. The conversations between these two friends, the irreverent expressions shock the conservative readers. Agastya expresses his disinterestedness towards his job which is rooted well in advance in his mind. Lack of seriousness towards his carrier indicates and mirrors the tendency of the modern Indian youth about the very occupation they need to do so. Amazing mix of the language makes the novel more interesting and connects to the real-life situation. On his first morning at Madna he felt like "fallen Adam' after being bitten by mosquitoes on cheeks, beards, ears, got his eyelids swollen and felt that Culcatta's mosquitoes seemed to be more civilized, they never touched the face. This place has drawn first blood, he thought, was not elephantiasis incurable?" (7) At Madna Agastya is accommodated in a Government Rest House, given the attendant Digamber and the cook Vasant who serves him insipid food. But Agastya remarks on the very first day. "Dinner was unbelievable, the dal tested like lukewarm chilled shampoo." (06) Later he says "...because at the rest house I seem to be eating Vasant's turds" (49). An element of black humor runs here when a bizarre and an unusual comparison takes place between face and food.

Another good sense of humor prevails through the description of the protagonist in the novel. Agastya himself laughs at his own suffering, tedium and displacement and the novelist says, "He realizes obscurely that he was to lead at least three lives in Madna, with its social concomitance, the unofficial, which included boozing with Shankar and Sathe, later with Bhatia, and the secret in the universe of his room which encompassed jigging by moonlight"

(48). Agastya's sense of aloofness makes him finding secret pleasure from doping, masturbating and boozing. This incident gives hilarious reference to his personal life and lies to everyone that he is twenty-eight years old and married of course; he wanted to say twice, though he is twenty four years old and still a bachelor. "She is in England. She is gone for cancer operation .She has cancer of the breast" (Chatterjee 14).

Again, the protagonist of the novel is quite casual and fabricates the stories soon. "Later in his training Agastya told the District Inspector of Land Records that his wife was a Norwegian Muslim." (15) Another fascinating and childhood experience once again amuse the readers when at school the English teacher asks about his ambition, Agastya writes in his essay that he wants to become a domesticated male stray dog because they live the best life. "They were assured of food, and because they were stray, they didn't have to guard a house or beg or shake paws or fetch trifles or be clean or anything similarly meaningless to earn their food" (36). Agastya is bit careless and turns the story according to his instinct. "His parents are in Antarctica, members of the first Indian expedition. Yes, even his mother; she had a PhD in Oceanography from the Sorbonne. After a while the personal questions stopped. Later he felt guilty, but only for a very brief while" (15).

Another delightful and light moment of the novel comes when Agastya is in the company of Superintendent of Police Mr. Dhiraj Kumar and lies that he has climbed Everest the previous summer. The protagonist is quite amusing and the author reveals laughter throughout the novel. Agastya feeds his personal details that fit to his mentality and tells differently to different persons about his marital status. When Mr. Kumar asks about his wife and her cancer he says, "I am not married, yet, sir. I would have been married long ago, but my father disapproves her, she's a Muslim" (110). Interestingly when Kumar recalls as heard that his wife was dying of cancer in England, Agastya says "Me? My wife? No, Sir, there is some confusion that's my cousin" (110) Later after few days S.P. Kumar asks "When are you getting married? Sen?" 'Not for a while'. He had forgotten that what story he had fabricated to Kumar" (Chatterjee 139).

The novelists employ the elements of comedy as an attack on the shortfalls of people society and human errors. Mark Twain remarks "Humor is the great thing, the saving thing after all. The minute it crops up, all our harnesses yield, all our irritations and resentments flit away and a sunny spirit takes their place." But the other kind of comedy that sometimes looks bizarre, freakish and shocking is called 'Black humor' or the term 'Black comedy'. According to the Random House Dictionary of English language, Black humor is a literary form that combines the morbid and grotesque with humor and farce to give a disturbing effect and convey the absurdity and cruelty of life. Encyclopedia defines the black humor as, 'writing that juxtaposes morbid or ghastly elements with comical ones that underscore the senseless or the futility of life.' Upamanyu Chatterjee employs his black comedy with a pinch of satire to make the protagonist Agastya and others expressing wry humor about the cynical ugly bewildering situations they come across. The author uses the technique like fragmented narration and different point of view and depicts wired and bizarre situations thus enabling the readers encounter frequent 'tongue in cheek' expressions which are amusing and entertaining.

Upamanyu Chatterjee published his novel English August: An Indian Story in 1988 and was filmed later on depicts Agastya Sen as a protagonist in the novel. Agastya is a city born and highly educated Anglophile and likes to be called 'August' or 'English'. His father and uncle call him 'Ogu' fondly. He lost his mother at his early age and his father is a retired IAS. Agastya is recruited to the Indian Administrative Service and is posted at Madna, as a trainee in an ugly, hot, small hinterland town of south India. But here Upamanyu Chatterjee adopts his technique of satire pinching a hole in the character of Agastya who is unable to adjust at Madna, uninterested in his job and reflects in an ironic way, comments silently at every situation in a tone of humor. The novel is all about the protagonist's experiences and reflections as a trainee at a small town where he feels dislocated, lives without any ambition or conviction, preoccupied by marijuana alcohol and sexual fantasies. After some encounters with his senior officers observing the dire living conditions of the tribal habitants, visiting a leper rehabilitation center he realizes his responsibilities and he is finally posted as Assistant Collector at Koltanga. Chatterjee has been successful in making the novel a lively satiric novel that mirrors the reflections of the modern urban educated youth and the lighter side of the affectation and pompous lifestyle of Indian bureaucrats.

Chatterjee's Fiction as the Expression of Stark Reality of the Society

The protagonist represents a disdainful youth, adolescence and successive growth. The entire plot of the novel vividly represents the socio-economic conditions of Indian citizen in some backwater hinterland. The fiction is the clear representation of the stark realities of India and the Indians, their typical lifestyles, of politicians, bureaucrats, businessmen, working class people and work culture in different walks of life. It represents the generation of the youth deviated from the disciplined life. Again, the Indian educated youth is under the whims of intoxication and abusive drugs. The protagonist confronts the clash between the oriental and occidental waves. The lethargic life style of Indian educated youth being detached from their inner conscience is a clear indicative of the alienated youth from the main stream. The novel delightfully narrates the typical Indian psyche and ideological issues as evident in the society. It is humorous, jovial, and frivolous raillery on the Indian social culture, societal institutions and politics.

The protagonist is a prototype of large number of Indian youth from urban area. Although he is an educated youth his tendency of nonexistence to the good morals is clearly visible in the very first appearance of the novel. The first paragraph contains some words like-*'time' 'stray dog', 'marijuana' and 'acute lethargy'* indicate the negation of the healthy positioning of Indian youth. Apart from this the condition of the youth is really shocking as they have been habituated by the slang language being affected by the western society. Dhruba, the closest friend to Agastya says, "I have a feeling

Agust, you are going to get hazar fucked in Madna." These slang languages significantly elaborate the fate and future of Indian youth on the crossroads of the society. The colonial power has already gone but the neo process of neo-colonialism is coming to front with its excessive impact of western cultural values. Indian ideological impact goes in vain.

Agastya's adolescence period is not fruitful as to expectation in Darjeeling who couldn't immerse himself into success. Rather Agastya was distinctively confined to a handful to his friend circle. Agastya and his friend Prashant were envious of the color of those "Anglo and Tib thighs" because it was 'not like theirs'. The novelist satires at the attitude of alienation from his own entity as he wished to be like Anglo-Indian having same look. Agastya gradually develops the desire to be an Englishman and also developed the tendency of soft drugs even in his school days. Agastya is not happy over his lucrative job, which every Indian aspires to get. But it is completely different for him. Agastya doesn't have curiosity, excitement and enthusiasm for this challenging job who feels him to be pushed under circumstantial compulsion. On his first train journey from Delhi to Madana, Agastya's mind is filled with strange feelings. He locks himself in the toilet and 'smoked some marijuana". At the very beginning of the training Agastya feels very awkward as he could not adjust to the reality at Madna and feels alienated. The "shabby stations of small towns, incurious patient eyes and weather-beaten bicycles at a level crossing, muddy children and buffalo at a water wholes pass behind his mind and he doesn't understand if he would be spending months in a dot in this hinterland"(4-5).The rural India with its typical "cigarette and pan dhabas, disliking food stalls, both lit by fierce kerosene lamps, cattle and clanging rickshaws on the road" etc. are disturbing elements as he is from metropolitan background.

A sense of self satisfactory pride reigns in the character of Dhrubo for earning a highest academic degree Ph.D from Yale but at the same time he forgets the past where he earned previous requisite qualification from India. Agastya's first day in district administration has been remarkable. According to him the district administration runs on the basis of tradition set during colonial period. The Britishers had set the principles. But it was Indianized afterwards. In postcolonial period the collector is accessible to every ordinary man. In fact, Agastya lacks this quality. The author remarks, "...administration is an intricate business, and a young officer who lacks initiative, cannot really be trained in its artifices. There is very little that he can learn from watching someone else, Agastya learnt nothing" (10). Zeal and enthusiasm were absent in Agastya. His mind is caught in some obscure and irrational.

An eminent critic Dr. Mukhul Dikshit opines that "Chattrerjee has, for the first time focused on the new class of westernized urban Indians that was hitherto ignored in the regional as well as English fiction of India" (Wikipedia). Humor takes of the ordinary characters or situations and exaggerates them far beyond the normal satire or irony. The satirists satirize even the great icons of the nation, religious beliefs and even the deeply rooted sentiments of the people. For instance Agastya observes the Gandhi Hall beside the police station of Madna and is bewildered at its dilapidated stage, its broken windows, old walls and it appears to him as a sight of a TV news clip of 'bomb- hit Beirut'. He asks the collector about the funny looking statue. At the interview for the post of teachers the education officer and the DDO Mr. Bajaj asks some questions to candidates. Agastya enters, joins them in the process. Agastya's entry made the situation solemn. Out of twenty-three candidates only six had turned up. Last candidate was called who was a graduate and mumbled the answers of the preliminary questions. "Then Bajaj asked who is called the father of nation? 'Nehru'. A pat reply. 'I see, and what is Gandhi then? Perhaps the uncle of the nation?' (88) He has an unerring touch and perfect balance to maintain continuous comic entertainment without ever descending into farce.

Most of Indian youths suffer from anxiety and insecurity in the society related to profession according to qualification. Ambition may not match to the expectation of the youth. There is a rising rate of unemployment among them. He has to compromise with his ego, identity and status. A sense of identity diffusion runs through the novels of Upamanyu Chatterjee. However, Agastya is undoubtedly very lucky to have accomplished most attractive job in this country. In fact, Agastya differs from others where he likes a secretive and complete freedom from any chains or restrictions.

7

Comic Portrayal of Power-Hungry Politicians in Anurag Mathur's *Making the Minister Smile*

Anurag Mathur is one of the towering literary figures in the postmodern Indian English fiction. As a significant writer Mathur's novels are expressions of most intimate conscious of life and society, which forms the impressive core of literature. Mathur's fictional world includes *Inscrutable Americans* (1991), *Making the Minister Smile* (1996), *The Department of Denials* (2004) and *The Country is Going to the Dogs* (2014).

Urmila Rao observes in The Hindu on Anurag Mathur's writings, "His writing effort is a disciplined regime of one to four in the morning unravels the novelist [...] And a significant part of the walking hours goes in the conscious effort of keeping track of the world, be aware of the happenings in politics, culture, society" (www.thehindu.com). Indeed, Mathur's writings are sharp satires with comic expressions to rectify the vices and follies of the society and individuals. Mathur's fictions are the guardian of ideals with corrective measures.

In support of comic situation in our daily life, our Prime Minister Mr. Narendra Modi addressing the 47th anniversary of Tamil Magazine Thuglak, considered humor as the 'best healer' and said the power of smile and laughter is more powerful than abuse or any other weapon. "Humor builds bridges instead of breaking them...And this is exactly what we require today. Building bridges,

bridges between people, bridges between communities, bridges between societies." (Narendra Modi)

Making the Minister Smile published in 1996 is a novel of Mathur which is a critique on the Indian way of life with serious reading. The whole story is about all a person has to do to make a minister smile. The novel looks at the Indian poverty, politics and its eccentricities from an outsider's point of view. This novel presents an accurate Indian political scene and the relation of business men with others, as appearing to a common man in India. The presentation of satire and humour got mixed up with a serious topic. The present novel takes off from where the previous novel, *The Inscrutable American* trailed. The earlier one was noteworthy for its delicate humor and distinctive style of Hinglish or as to say that English that most of Indians speak. The present one is about a football player from America, Chris Stark and his exploration in India. Stark's family has business partnership with the company of Ram Avtar Kapoor in India and the young American is here to get the first-hand know-how about the labor problems crippling KapCo, Kapoor's company.

Making the Minister Smile is a novel about the adventures of an American among the inscrutable Indians. Chris Stark, an American arrives in India for commercial purpose. Chris, father owned 'Stark Plastics', a plastic company, comes to east for the collaboration with KapCo in India. However, in India Chris faces exceptional situations caused from industrial disputes and political machinations with other oddities. Labour problem brings a great obstacle in front of Chris. The minister in the name of Mani Shankar Aiyar is indifferent and callous to the real problem. Chris turns to be a victim who confronts power hungry politician and finds himself astounded in globalizing India.

The fiction is an excellent portrayal of the underbelly of the Indian political system and the notion that Crish experiences as an observer participant. Kapoor tries hard to persuade the workers but becomes unproductive. Kapoor's principle of three 'Butter them, bribe them or Bash them' have proved to be ineffective. Frustrated

Kapoor meets Sevak Chand, the minister in charge of the department concerned. The strike starts and the hard work of the management to shatter are worthless. Prabal Kumar leads the strike. Astonishingly the police, stationed there do nothing as Kumar's men bash up the loyal workers who try to enter the factory. The secretary informs that unless Kappoor make the minister smile there was not much hope to bring change. From then Kapoor tries to find a way to make the minister smile and it makes very funny reading. *Making the Minister smile* is about the adventures of an average American among the inscrutable Indians. An American football player comes to the mystic East, that is India, Delhi to further business links between his plastic manufacturing company in a small town of America and the KapCo Company of Delhi. While in India the protagonist Chris Stark becomes enmeshed in industrial disputes, political intrigues, wired intelligence webs and an unfortunate love affair besides various other oddities. The owners of Indian Delhi based company called KapCo, the well-connected Kapoors of Punjabi Bagh, bribe, bash and butter all those who can bring ministerial favors to squash a rampaging union leader; the minister is satisfyingly vulpine, complete with hooded eyes and Nehruvian references, who only smiles. And then there is a devil himself travelling under the name of Mani Shankar Aiyar, who lurks behind buses but then revealed to be a Pakistani agent. Crish Stark , steak and apple-pie-soccer player, finds himself astounded by globalizing India far into anything confronted with the estate of unknowing on whose brink New India stands.

This book starts with a comic note but drifts to a something a serious labour problem. The time was glorious winter afternoon in New Delhi. Green grass, blooming flowers, gentle sunshine and Mr. Sundaran speaking English before Christopher shortly named as Crish who is perhaps gets surprise at the reaction of Sundaran. A good humor runs here. "Ouch, winced Chris. He wondered what had disturbed Mr. Sunder so deeply. Perhaps a potato had been found to be rotten. Or a tomato to be pulpy. Or perhaps even horrors, the meat to be a day old." (01) Humor is the most effective literary weapon to please the audience. The skill fits the writing of

Anurag Mathur here. The reader's nerves got relaxed when Chris faced inscrutable Indian in India with feelings of awe and mystery. Chris faced an Indian's continuous cough and spitting blood into the dustbin and thinks that the guy got tuberculosis. Chris hesitated to breathe and surprises at the consequence of coming to India. "When Chris reached him, the man coughed gratingly, gargled loudly and spat a thick wad of blood into a bin. Chris recoiled. 'Shit' he thought, 'the boy got tuberculosis.' He tried not to breathe. Jesus, fifteen minutes in India and I am going to be infected with TB, he thought holding himself rigid." (04)

Christopher Morley (1890-1957) in *The Power of Sympathy* (1923) quotes on humor that, "Humor is perhaps a sense of intellectual perspective: an awareness that something's are really important, others not; and that the two kinds are most oddly jumbled in everyday affairs." Again, Chris gets bewilderment at the strange behavior of the luggage which got missing when was with Ajai and compares America to India. All the life in America he had idea that bags were just bags. They lay there, you fill them up with things and then you carried them about whenever you went. If you put them somewhere they stayed put. They are peaceful in inanimate companions. But in India, they miraculously came to life, taking on the magic, mystery and personality of frisky elves. (06) KapCo had an intense labor problem which is to be taken seriously. Mathur has used his skill with apt care and attention of the common man's problems in our society. It's is hard to concentrate on personal demand when you are trying to adjust to a cow contentedly chewing the cud in the middle of an intensely crowded street. He had found nobody else paying the slightest attention to the animal and began to feel that perhaps he was a little peculiar in noticing the sight" (07). Chris again gets astonishment at the diversity of Indian society particularly traffic. Chris recalls a Lebanese friend telling him that there was an ice field around Americans. But in India Chris feels that the sunshine perhaps has melted that ice. Pollution is a great problem in India and overcrowded population facilitates this problem to a great extent. Mathur presents the real condition in the fiction. "The dust and the fumes had annoyed him the most. But seeing the commercial frenzy on the sidewalks; he had decided that the priorities were first to do business and later to look into the problems caused by pollution" (09). The union leaders were asking for unreasonable demands. Political corruption was a major theme in the novel. Chris enters Ajai Vir's room. Another comic incident comes to add to the situation finding a tall blackboard with B.B.B written on it in chalk. Ajai Vir erases it every morning and writes it again so that he remembers for the rest of the day. Chris is perplexed at the meaning of it. Interestingly Ajai explains it that butter them, bribe them or bash them. "Butter them. Bribe them or Bash them. 'Perfect, applauded Chris, 'The Havard Business School couldn't teach you better" (11).

The head of KapCo's security, Capt.A.S.Singh joins the company after retiring from army is in uneasiness at the chanting mob through the grilled window of office adjacent to the office gate. Capt. Singh informs Lal Verma, manager of the factory of the problem. Mr. Verma gets the hot line telephone and wants to talk to the Kapoor sahib directly. But Mr. Sunder on other side convinced him to pass the message as Kapoor sahib was in prayer. He doesn't like Mr. Verma really. However, Mr. Sundere changed dramatically when he got bad news about the strike by the workers and didn't like to be a carrier of bad news at all. Suddenly he changed his stand. "I'll get him on the phone right way" said Mr. Sunder who had long ago learned it was wiser not to be the carrier of bad news" (18).

One of the funniest comments like 'All men may be animals, but all women are animal lovers' comes from Anurag Mathur. The first and the wittiest modern writer that we have today deserve a lot of attraction. Mathur's graceful style with politically correct argument has earned him a worldwide reputation and acclaim in the world. In a short time, he has captured a wide range of place in the heart of the readers. The author's razor-sharp sense of humor makes us conscious about simple but important issues which have always been unnoticed as trivial or quite unimportant. Mathur's simple reference to bags disappearing in India but staying put in

America is quite amusing and creates a sense of laughter. It not only entertains but also brings us the hard truths of our Indian society. Indian politicians are typical in the sense of making promise to the people. They don't care of the general public. Their false promises and hypocrisies come to the fore interestingly. Usually, they strive to sustain their vote bank policy instead of looking the issues carefully. Chris comes to India as a result of his family's Corporation's collaboration an Indian company. But in India he becomes entangled with industrial disputes and it got worse when there is political meddling. Jaychandran, an eminent critic observes that the solution to the entire Gordian knot of problems in the novel is making the minister smile. The novel presents an accurate Indian political scene as it appears to a common man in India. Some of critics appear at times that Mathur makes an unfair comparison between India and United States of America. But it is true that Mathur definitely makes an effort to convey the message to the readers. In fact Mathur satirizes the future politicians of this country with a note of caution with firm convictions about the politicians; trade unions and Indian work culture are unique in the sense of satire with a pinch of humor.

Mathur gives a picture of Indian's rich people are careless in arranging dinners in various occasions. Chris refuses the offer of attending dinner by Sharmaji and gets surprise at the attitude of rich Indians. Chris wondered, "How anyone could believe that India was full of starving people." (34)

There was violence because of labor problems and strike. When Ram Avtar mentioned violence, the minister dragged Gandhiji and said, "Let us eschew violence" (68). Naturally like other Indian politicians he continued that "The law will take its own course" (69).

The story revolves round the disagreement surrounding the company and its workers union. The workers, the union leaders and the management endeavor to reach at the harmonious solution rather they fail to resolve the factory problem. The author succeeds in maintaining his sardonic sense of humor. For instance, the way

Chris is shocked when he meets Kalpana Singh who shatters the image of perfect Indian girl he had in mind, one who symbolizes chastity and innocence is hilarious. Taken as a whole, Making the Minister is full of amusement, wit and surprises with a subtle touch of satire. It takes a close look at the corruption which is rampant in the Indian political circles and establishments. Mathur's sarcastic sense of humor is much entertaining.

In the midst of problems among the workers police was silent on the violence. When Ram Avtar, Ajai and Khris asked Sharmaji about the incident he said clearly that "The minister didn't mention about protecting the workers. He mentioned as per Nehru's wishes, about protecting the factory" (Mathur 65). The Minister Sevak Chand was a typical leader who gives a ministerial remark when Ram Avtar introduced Chris. Sevak Chand took the reference of then PM's words, "Foreign collaborations are most welcome and will bring prosperity to both parties and our great countries" (66). At the news the massacre appeared, and Prabal Kumar became the head of the leading trade unions most of the political partics starts to compete to invite him and get associated with. Prabal on the other hand said, "I have no ambitions becoming a political leader. I am only interested in serving the toiling worker whose labor creates wealth for the proprietor and the country, but who is himself denied a fair share of the fruits of his toil"(74).In course of events the problems still continues. Ajai decided to finish Prabal with the help of politicians and gundas. Ajai told Chris, "We need not a politician but a thug" (166).

At last Ram Avtar Kapoor takes the way to find the minister smile. In a press conference Verma welcomed everyone and announced, "We had given all the deep thoughts to all the demand and based upon what we feel is fair and just both to workers and KapCo and according to the wage structure that is prevalent all over India, we have come to a decision" (210).

8

The Comic Vision in Anurag Mathur's *Inscrutable Americans*

The connection between literature and life is vital and intimate. It creates the way to express their thoughts and ideas while the subject matter and treatment must be such as of general interest and the expression must be emotive that gives pleasure and satisfaction to the readers. Humor and satire are the two distinct elements of literature and are considered staple of it. They are the key ingredients of life or a good read. Without humor literature is tasteless curry with no spice. People of all ages and cultures respond to humor. A few writers in the galaxy of Indian writings are there who have left their footprints in this way to create a light moment for the burdened hearts. One such bright example is Anurag Mathur's *Inscrutable Americans*. The fiction is an incredible account of a small-town boy caught in the attractive, mysterious, inexplicable whirl of the great United States of America where sex, alcoholism and women are very common. The present paper aims to explore the humorous elements with pun intended in many situations.

The history of Indian English novel is incomplete without the contribution of Anurag Mathur. He was born in New Delhi and educated at Sindia School (Gwalior), St Stephens College (Delhi) and University of Tulsa (Oklahoma). He spent three years in USA and has been successful in creating a number of literary masterpieces. Mathur's literary works include *Inscrutable Americans* (1991), *Making the Minister Smile* (1996), *The Departments of the Denials* (2004) and recently published *The Country is Going to the Dogs*

(2014) have impacted the readers with its hilarious elements with use of satire. Mathur's *Inscrutable Americans* is an all-time best seller since its debut in 1991 and for the long eleven years notwithstanding media hype and success stories surrounding other books. On Mathur's present fiction Nikhil Mukhija comments, "as the very name suggests is a story about Americans where a talented boy Gopal goes to the west to pursue diploma [...], is tempted by culture there and tries to gel in under the guidance of friend Randy who takes a pledge to make him experience all the pleasures of an American lifestyle".

Humor is the genre that if executed well brings a sense of relief even to the tired minds. Mathur's present novel is a charming and hilarious story about Gopal, a simple chap is the heart of the story. As a young man from the small town of India, Jajau and a son of a hair oil businessman in Madhya Pradesh arrives in America to study chemical engineering in a university in Evers vile for graduation that forms the crux of the story. The fiction is a comical take on the lives of Americans. As Gopal reaches New York he is reccived by Sunil and Sushant and his comic discovery of America starts. The author contrasts the cultural differences with references based on humour and satire. Gopal comes to America with pre-conceived notion. Gopal's English is hilarious and the simple character's ignorance and innocence and point-blank honesty are attractive and at the same time the readers are taken aback by how minute details from day-to-day life of Americans amaze him. Gopal's reactions to the climate the people, malls etc. have been described through the words of the mouth Gopal's take on sex and the ways of Americans in general are amusing and entertaining. Gopal is seen as a person who is torn between his urges and the values inculcated in him by his parents. The author has clearly brought out the differences between the two cultures via humor and simplicity.

Despite all the 'Dos and Don'ts' that his family imposes upon him Gopal is tempted by the culture there and tries to get under the guidance of Randy who takes pledge to make him experience all the pleasures of American living. The letters, Gopal writes back to his younger brothers in India takes the readers to a laughter ride. The book like a young Indian man's dream of what Americans are like with a university student level twist on global geo politics. There he battles the usual issues faced by an Indian living like racism. Sexual discomforts, food etc.

The novel starts with the letter by Gopal to his younger brother describing his experiences in the American heartland. The hometown Jajau is known as the 'Paris of Madhya Pradesh' but didn't get much exposure to the rest developed parts of the world. Barely having any contact with girls, much less intimate with one. The story takes place through his eyes, his thoughts and views of life. Gopal's very first letter gets the readers start laughing at his English and its structure of sentences. The letter is written in Indian English being extremely humorous and entertaining. "Beloved Younger Brother,

> "Greetings to Respectful parents' .I am hoping all is well with health and wealth. I am fine at my end. Hoping your end is fine too. With God's grace and parent's Blessings I am arriving safely in America and finding good apartment near university..." (1). In the globalized world Gopal lags behind to others and has doubts on the cooks and their caste that whether they are Brahmins or not. "I am strictly consuming vegetarian only in the restaurants though I am not knowing if the cooks are Brahmins" (01).

A good sense of humor runs through the readers when Gopal the protagonist is bewildered out of his simplicity. He gets surprised about the people of America. "I am not knowing where to start. Most surprising thing about America is that it is full of Americans, Americans big and white..." (01). Another hilarious situation comes through Gopal's obnoxious notion on English understanding ability of the air-hostess. Gopal thinks him superior to them which are indeed contrary to the reality. "I think perhaps she is not understanding proper English" (10). Mathur's description of the New York City will flash right in front of the reader's eyes. Through this letter Mathur again attempts to create light moments when Gopal gets excitement over the lights in New York and feels that as if God has created a carpet of lights over the town. At the time of landing from the aero plane the air-hostess offered him a cane of Coca-Cola with a smile. The innocent chap doesn't understand it. This short glance of behavior with smile changes his previous notion of Americans. "I think they are knowing everything about everybody who is coming to America" (11).

Simplicity through the protagonists prevails most of time and creates laughter. Gopal's first friendship with Joe, a Negro gentle man makes him feel very close and infers him to be treated properly by his parents, if he comes to Jajau. Gopal faces an immigration officer when conceives as the American having information of the visitors before. Gopal instructs his brother to lock all doors and windows. Interestingly Gopal conceives them as CIA agents having information even about their donkey. "But brother, now I am worrying. Supposing this is CIA keeping watch or else how they can know about our donkey." (12) Once again simplicity and honesty prevail in the character of Gopal who doesn't want to cheat his motherland. American beauty has impressed him and looks desperately a beautiful lady on the way with Sushant and Sunil. Gopal was unable to understand the mystery of the basket that was hung in front of every house and thought it to be connected with the religion but resolved not to ask anybody apprehending to be proved as silly and foolish.

The protagonist discovers a part of New York on the way to the airport from where a certain amount of confusion starts right from the American girls, new gadgets and the naked billboards. Again Gopal gets puzzled over the vegetarian cats and continues with the telephone and color TV with various channels. Gopal meets Randy who welcomes at the airport and introduces to the American society and the way of living. Randy helps him to his destination. Gopal feels sleepy and at the same time, thinks about his homeland. The novelist here tries to present another hilarious situation as the innocent chap is concerned about the name Randy and compares to Randy's meaning in India and feels that he got a friend at last but to him only girls are Randy; maybe Randy is one of those boy types. "He said he is randy. I know from penthouse letters about that, but there are only girls are randy. Maybe he is one of those boys' types. I must be careful." Next morning, Gopal is sleepily awake, looks around through gummy eyes and struggled up wondering where he was. He is worried about what lay ahead and compares most of Americans as monsters. "Monsters with American faces materialized in front of him waiting to perform unimaginable cruelties."

Another comic reference comes out from the friendship of Randy and Gopal. Randy comments on a girl, Mary Lou. Gopal asks about the girl. Randy lightly compares her to the Linda Lovelace of the campus. Interestingly Gopal remarks him as the Harry Reems. By the way they reached at the Administration building. A short and a red-haired man, Dean Smith infers him to be Gopal. When he asks him his name and said that Randy must be looking after. When he asked that abut the discussion at that very moment Gopal immediately mentioned the name of Linda Lovelace. With beautiful skill of humor Mathur has tried to create light moments for the readers. "You must be Gopal"; "I am Dean Smith. I hope Randy's been looking after you. What was he telling you about just now?"; "Linda Lovelace Sir" (37). Randy gurgled. Dean Smith gave him an old-fashioned look as they went up the stairs.

Smith was bit caring to Gopal and instructs Randy to show Gopal library, bookstore, help him to meet teachers and show him the classrooms. Being a simple chap Gopal conceives him as very friendly. Contrary to the notion, Randy makes him cautious about the future possibility of getting low grades. A sense of difference makes the situation hilarious. On the other hand Randy asks him to wait for the result and says that he is different as to his appearance. "He is friendly" Gopal told Randy as they went down the staircase. "Yeah, but not always. Wait till you get bad grades once you would think you would murder his mother, the way he is carries on." (39) Gopal gets bewildered over the sharing of same bathrooms both by boys and girls. Again, he is obsessed with white beauty and feels the difference between the west and east. He is stunned over the American mall and huge doubled storied building. Gopal's repeated letter to his brother is full of entertaining and hilarious. The language he uses is very attractive and eye catching. He describes his new experience there about America and her people. "Beloved youngest one, "how much I am missing one and all I simply cannot say. My head is eating circles" (54). Gopal writes about the lack of Brahmins in America and also mentions that America is full of divorcees and assures his brother avoiding them. Again, he noticed a girl greeting him. But baffled and confused Gopal is bit reluctant to greet him same way. Rather he was not expecting such greeting from any girl. The novelist tries utmost care to ease and relax the reader's minds. "Hi," said the startled voice. "Gopal was equally shocked, but recovered on seeing the girl with the kind face. He dug his hands into his overcoat and beamed awkwardly at her." "I am friend of Randy, "he explained in a rush in case she was planning to throw him out" (69). Gopal gets a chance to dance with a girl Ann but finds uneasy to match with others. In spite of his lose interest in it Gopal gets closer to the girl and thinks do describe his friends in India about the closeness with beautiful girl. "Gopal could scarcely believe it. What a good time he was having. What a story to tell his friends when he got home.........And he would tell them about this lovely girl....and how she had grabbed the leg –he would show them the spot, a pity he could brand her fingerprints as a proof then taken him by the hand and dragged him into a dark room to dance" (75).

Gopal writes in the next letter about aloofness towards the American way of life and asks his brother not tell about every odd there lest she would bother. Gopal is surprised to see washing machine there. "Also, brother, you are not telling mother, but they are machines here that are cleaning clothes and drying in jiffy. I am knowing about all things and handling with mastery. My clothes are washing whitest and finger licking good" (80). Contrary to his writing Gopal is exposed to the American way of life. While we move into the next course of events, we see Gopal's preferences and thought process changes as he exposed more and more. Gopal goes with Randy to real bar and asks for cigarette.

Mathur again presents a comic situation in portraying the simplicity in Gopal when Gopal writes letter to his brother that he is going to buy TV from Safeway. Gopal mentions that they are known earlier and just like his friends and can ask discount and questions that how can they be friends if they are not giving discount? "Any way what to do but at least my new TV is coming yesterday, which I am buying from Safeway. I wish I am knowing earlier that they are my friends right down the street so that I can ask for discount otherwise how they are my friends?"(78)In course of events Gopal comes in contact with beautiful ladies at the bar. When she asks about her dance and asks to buy some drink honey his head moves vigorously and thinks to be ready to buy the empire state building if she asks for. "Oh yes Gopal's head moved vigorously. As a matter of fact he was going to buy the empire state building for her if she asked for it" (94).

All the letters Gopal writes to younger brother is complained about the language and the inability to understand resulting in awkward situations. "Any way I am learning many important things about Americans. Biggest thing is language. It is earlier making many problems for me, because like everyone I am thinking Americans are speaking English, it is American. I am facing so many embarrassing on this reason." (189) Mathur satirizes at the American student's lack of interest in utilizing the opportunity available there through beautiful characterization of Gopal. In another occasion Gopal meets Sue while returning from library. He is highly impressed by the emotion shown by her, but his heart breaks when he discovers Sue with another man. Disappointed Gopal now spends time by drinking and vomiting. Gopal again discovers the white supremacy over the blacks as he comes to know the actual poverty among them.

Gopal is subjected to the traditional method of education where everything got drilled into his mind by the route system of learning where questioning was heresy by the teachers. With perfect skill of satire, the novelist tries to induce satire here. Gopal's thought process revolves round in America leading to blooming out and learning the art of logical thinking, deductive reasoning and most important of all encompassing thirst for knowledge. Respect for teachers was really high now seems old bigoted people. Through the character of Gopal the author forays into the Indian psyche of malice and jealousy which are unnoticed in American society. There are several instances where Gopal's gentle innocence leads him to pretty hilarious conclusion. When he is asked to watch his ass "watch your ass" that leads Gopal quickly assumes that the man was referring to his two donkeys that his family had bought before his departure from India. The comic description really is heart touching. Gopal wonders how they know of the two donkeys, and believes that it is the part of the bigger conspiracy of the CIA collecting all the data that they can have idea about everyone coming to America. Again, Gopal sees himself as a cultural ambassador and the way he sets intention is quite amusing and thinks that because of India's superior culture they must set an example so that the American must improve their behavior leading to bilateral relationship. Gopal's character has a rustic undertone while others are characterized by the American ways of thinking as far as food, women and dating are concerned. The novel is a story of comic satire on the stereotypes and prejudices of Indian migrants in their adopted land. Gopal interacts with Tom. Gopal says all are same and stresses that Indians are like this. Tom is surprised "Yes. Yes everywhere people are same. I am having uncle who is so proud of India and culture that he is thinking all are inferior." "India has a culture? "Here Mathur satirizes at the American insularity and ignorance of other culture.

Gopal's day to day activities in the alien culture and social surrounding seems ludicrous who faces with pretty issues, encounters some shocking people and his bewilderment towards the diverse culture. Again, the funny Indian references make it more attractive. In spite of criticism the novel grasps its position well. The novel may not be for hardcore literature lovers but it is good for the persons who have penchant for comedy.

At last Gopal's one year of spending in America comes to an end and Gopal departs from America taking with him memories of alien culture. The best moment of the novel comes when Gopal comes in contact with a lady in the plane and starts discussing with her and his adventures with women in a diverse and powerful country in America. Gopal also mentions the uninteresting future in India and an unknown wife and feels engrossed by her and they suddenly start kissing each other while talking. At last, his dream comes to be true and is fulfilled which is fulfilled at least above 30,000 feet above the ocean. Gopal feels that he is satisfied and has become a man.

After all the novel is a cute, charming, hilarious and poignant novel that heels the burdened minds of the readers and a sensitive portrayal of the tribulations of the first time in America from India and how the protagonist tries to retain self-esteem and identity there. The letters are full of laughter which adds smiles to a great number of faces. Gopal the village boy's innocence has been portrayed quite convincingly and the obsession with Jajau's Hair Oil Factory is much funny and comic. The author captures the immigrant experiences of culture clash in a different way that attract huge number of students. This novel brings out the striking features of the diverse cultures with doses of laughter. Gopal's attempts to understand the American culture with the help of his mentor is quite amusing and funny. The comic vision in the novel is well articulated. It's quite funny and worth reading and brings a sense of relief to the readers. Comic relief, the chief ingredient of a good read is presented through the novelist's beautiful skill. The author manages to maintain the flow of the story admirably. The book is pleasure to read. A pinch of communism and racism add flavor to the comic elements making it cuter, sweet and light read. It is a non-stop ride in hilarity.

9

A Satirist as the Guardian of Ideals in Anurag Mathur's *The Country is Going to the Dogs*

Anurag Mathur's fictions are deliberately fun intended. As far as humor quotient is concerned Anurag Mathur tries to make the most of the situations in his fifth novel *The Country is going to the Dogs*. The novel is light hearted in its tone and seeks to attain its objective to create laughter among the readers from its very outset. Published in 2014 the novel attracts a huge number of students and seems a humorous novel with a great deal of satire. It's a critique on the Indian mindset of modernism and conservatism. Mathur has spent three years in the United States and comes up with a theme which grazes the cultural conflict between two societies which according to him is the class conflict between our conservative traditional upbringing and the new India. Mathur's novels are pun oriented and the humor is subtly incorporated.

The story revolves round Mr. Radhey Radhey who is also known as RR. As the protagonist RR takes up the assignment to find Miss Fifoo, the so-called sex siren of the sin city Delhi. She has gone missing. RR, seventy-four-year-old is a retired government accountant and lives just across the street of the All-Saints Women College. He has retired as a senior officer in the accounts department of the government of India and has started a small accounting practice in one room soot of the three-room place which was bought after his retirement. The readers are introduced Radhey Radhey as the protagonist who is having doubled standard thinking and his incessant moral policing. RR feels disgusted with woman wearing tight clothes making sex appeals to others but at the same time tries to reflect the wide spread mentality of the Indian men. Despite being critical, RR casts his eyes on the girls and he was always pleased to see them. The novelist uses a perfect example of satire here.

> Such tight, tight jeans" he criticized. So tight that if he looked hard enough, he could see the outline of the underwear. Nor that I would ever look so hard." He assured himself. "And such tight –T shirts. Goodness me, they may as well not even wear them. But in my days …ah in my days women knew how to dress, how to walk, how to talk, but now it was all sex, sex and nothing else (01).

Unlike other bureaucrats RR has not made much money from his practice, since a lifetime in government service had made him incapable of pushing for work. The novelist has satirized the Indian bureaucrats in fact. Usually most of them are corrupt and practice wrong way to congregate money RR gets assignment from the principal Mrs. Malhotra to find out the missing girl, Miss Fifoo, famous film star and one of the most famous old students of the college. The writer beautifully describes the two sides of RR's life. RR is ready to assist Mrs. Malhotra to find out the missing girl. After retirement most of the officers remain away from the busy life but RR just differs to them.

Again the author has attempted to present day reality through various situations. When RR is offered help to take the assistance of any one, he wants; RR immediately takes the name of beautiful Tia which creates a ludicrous situation in the course of the novel. Instead, Mrs. Malhotra rejects his intention of being relaxed by the presence of this beautiful girl. Rather she asks him to take help from Goburdhunji, the proprietor and editor of The Daily Reporter. Mr. Goburdhunji is presented as a character of major figure of power of the city influencing the fall and rise of the government. The role of the media is aptly presented. RR is of dual mentality and thinks of Tia, the most beautiful girl and a chance of interacting with her. RR is in search of the opportunity of talking with them if situation permits. "Besides, in the process he would interact with people from the college, especially with Tina. And if not her, then at least with the students, whose freshness and gaiety and enthusiasm so enlivened his slow and boring life and enriched his rapidly declining years" (07).

RR asks Goburdhun about the employees and reply in a disgusting manner. The present state of the course of the novel aptly expresses the plight of the ill mentality of the employees. Most of them are opportunists. At this very moment RR is desperate and shows his feelings that create a comic situation in the novel. Being the forerunner of Chetan Bhagat, Mathur tries hard to make light moments for the readers. "The nation has gone to the dogs," he concurred. It's all crimes and crowds and scams. And you people have no respect for their elders. I mean, look at the way the girls dress. Sometimes I feel like catching hold of them and dressing them myself" (Mathur 09).

Humour is a funny thing. It can crack you up unexpectedly or it can make the entire movie hall full of laughter. But in fact, they are short in supply. The present novel tries to minimize the gap to some extent. RR is an innocent in the wilderness acquaints himself in the sexual underbelly of Delhi while uncovering the mystery of the missing girl.

Some of the characters RR comes across during his investigation are quite interesting. For instance, the veteran crime reporter Anwar helps him at every point. The story revolves round where RR found himself in the car heading towards the police headquarters being taken by Anwar, the crime reporter of 'The Daily Reporter.' Shelley Sahib known as poetic pimp creates many light moments for the readers and continues his supremacy and impact in the sexual underworld that makes RR to comment in a comic and satiric way. He asserts that the country is going to the dogs as everyone is drowning in sex. "Anwar smirked. They are dime a dozen have them. Every city, every town, every district sometimes even villages have them. Its sex, sex and sex, the whole country is drowning in sex" (Mathur 23). Through typical citation of different poems from English literature makes the novel more humorous. Shelly remains pleased at the outrageous flattery of him. Anwar makes his great telling that he is the great example of democratic way of functioning. "Shelly Bhai. You are well known for your democratic way of functioning. You have even won an award for running a flat organization. You are fine example globally. The world knows and admires you" (27).

The next few days RR's mind keeps repeating in disbelief when RR comes to know about 'wife swapping' in the land of Mahatma Gandhi. Interestingly he had double mentality and his mind was in ferment to have ideas that what really goes at such places. Comical and confused attitude towards sex and its various manifestations are prevalent in the fiction through the character RR. "What went on such places.... RR's mind was in ferment. How did it work? Could anyone come with their wives, or it was a group of friends? If it was a group of friends, how could he attend? I certainly have no friends I could invite along for a wife-swapping party. I have led a decent, middle class, conservative life; he talked aloud to calm himself down" (29).

Unlikely people from the present generation, RR hesitates to become a part of the sinister activity like wife swapping and concludes to be the bottom part of this. "This is clearly something sinister that the younger generation is up to, something quite unknown to my age group, and I have to get to the bottom of this" (30). Again the novelist also satires at the doubled standards of Mr.RR when he mentions that RR gets himself ready for the wife swapping party in spite of his unwillingness. None the less, he got himself a new set of clothes, shoes and underwear. Not because he was planning anything unIndian but because, he reasoned, one must put one's best foot forward at all times. Once again Mathur hits at his best skill of satirizing the protagonist and his mentality. RR is surprised at the intention of wife swapping party and especially a girl like Tina and her boldness to become a participant. But at the same time, he is soft towards her prettiness. "And what was this Tina girl like? He pondered with even more excitement. What kind of woman would agree to go with a total stranger to be exchanged there with a greater stranger? She must be very bold. But what is she like, as a person / I simply must find out? Not that I plan to see her again. No, no. But is she friendly? Is she at least pretty? (32)

Interestingly RR noted the beauty and elegance of such beautiful girl Tina. RR compares his baldness with the acute beauty and is glad that at least he has bought a new pair of clothes and has used profuse quantity of aftershave cologne that he rarely uses otherwise. "RR noted her beauty, her elegance, her obvious sophistication and acutely felt the baldness of his head, with its covering of thin long strands that he had slicked down with Brycreem. He was glad that he had bought an entirely new set of clothes and had used profuse quantities of cologne that he rarely used otherwise" (32). RR finds it difficult to digest the worst situation to have such a pity and unacceptable tradition of wife swapping in the capital city of India and deeply regrets over such nefarious activities and surprises at the permission by the central government of India only ten kilometers of the parliament, the most sacred and august house. "I must alert the government, was his last thought as he fell into a deep sleep. Our nation has gone to the dogs" (Mathur 41).

Another comic situation is created when RR is frustrated over the failure of the present bureaucrats to stop nefarious activities in the society in a hilarious way, he advises Anwar to invite retired people to run this country. "They have messed up the corporate sector and now they want to mess up the govt. also. This country has no future. They should bring back the retired people to run the country" (Mathur 44).

The process of looking for the clues to find the actress, RR again comes to meet the situation that the young people are so ardent to have lost time even in front of others. Although RR finds hard to digest, still remembers his past having the same. RR recalls past about kissing and hugging with a neighbor's wife which is in fact satirized by the novelist. Again, images of Laxmi forced him spend sleepless nights and tossed and turned remembering the shape of her legs, the curve of her bottom. "He couldn't sleep that night. Images of Laxmi, that was her name overpowered his senses. He tossed and turned as he remembered the shape of her legs, the curve of her bottom" (63).

However, *The Country is Going to the Dogs* follows the exploits of a 74-year-old through various stages to find out Miss Fifoo. A self-declared Gandhian provides a funny firsthand account as he is thrown out of his comfort zone. RR is forced to rub his shoulder with gangsters and eunuchs. Mathur brings out the hypocrisy of RR interestingly and effectively. There are times when the readers rise at him with sympathy but there are times when they scream at him for being complete hypocrite. There are rapid series of events in the novel. Mathur has been successful to introduce a series of very interesting characters ranging from head strong independent homosexual activists to poetic Pimps who quote classic English poetry and a resourceful journalist Anwar who ends up being RR's side-kick in the adventures. RR belongs to the older generation who has really an ambivalent attitude towards sex. As a society we are very oversexed. Such a peculiar character creates laugh. Mathur says that RR is an imagination of a series of very confused characters; I have met who are very attracted by this new wave of sexuality and yet are very reluctant to accept it because of the way they have been culture and brought up.

Anurag Mathur has bagged wide acclamation throughout the world creating a separate place in the Indian English literature as a novelist. Mathur's novels are full of laughter, with social satire. The fictions of Mathur are expression of sardonic sense of humor. Apart from this Mathur's novels unfold the issues of power-hungry politicians and bureaucrats in India. Through various characters coming from different stratum Mathur aims to rectify the society, individuals and public authority in true sense. Most of his novels are charming, hilarious and poignant with sensitive portrayals of characters. Mathur's comic visions in his fictional narratives give relief to the readers. Mathur's novels are full of diverse culture with doses of laughter.

10

Humour as the Heart of Literature in Chetan Bhagat's *Half Girlfriend*

Humor is the sensitivity of literature that provokes laughter and provides amusement. As the main ingredient, humor intends to induce enjoyment, breaks the dullness, boredom, tiresomeness and makes the audience's nerves relaxed. George Meredith (1828-1909) in his *Essay on Comedy and the Uses of Comic Spirit* (1877) considers as the excellent test of the civilization of a country to be "the flourishing of comic idea and comedy" and it is of the true comedy that "it shall awaken thoughtful laughter" (Meredith 140). David Lubar an author of humorous books rightly remarks that "Humor brings pleasure, eases pain and makes the world a better place." People of all ages respond to humour and satire. "The satirist presupposes an educated readership which will easily be able to discover the implicit morality without any help other than a few ironic hints from the writer." In fact, they are short in supply. This paper aims at exploring Chetan Bhagat's *Half Girlfriend* in terms of its tone of humor and satire. In almost all his fictions, Chetan Bhagat has captured his deep concern about the adolescence in a comic and satiric way. Mark Taiwan (1835-1910), a great humorist, entrepreneur and publisher rightly remarks that "Humor is mankind's greatest blessing." He also satirizes the so-called beliefs and traditions of the society. Bhagat's present fiction *Half Girlfriend* sets the story of how Madhav Jha from backward Bihar is in pursuit of winning over the girl that he likes. Throughout the novel, the author has given the utmost attempt to create laughter among the readers. In fact, it's true that through humorous descriptions, Bhagat has shaped many Indians to develop reading habits.

Chetan Bhagat has revolutionized the Indian writing and has stormed into the literary landscape of Indian English literature. Born on 22nd April 1974, Bhagat is an immortal name in the history of Indian English literature. As a columnist, author, screenwriter, television personality and motivational speaker Bhagat has acclaimed a wide range of popularity in India. Bhagat's fictional world includes *Five Point Someone* (2004), *One Night @the Call Centre* (2005), *The Three Mistakes of my Life* (2008), *2 States: The Story of My Marriage* (2009), *Revolution 2020* (2011), *What Young India Wants* (2012), *Half Girlfriend* (2014), *Making India Awesome* (2015) and *One Indian Girl* (2016). Bhagat's Half Girlfriend is a hilarious and heart touching novel among the readers.

This unlikely writer in an engineer turned investment banker made light fiction ever-present enough to adorn the selves of book stores across the country. The author needs to be praised for the humorous elements that are predominant frequently in the novel. The back cover page of Bhagat's *Half Girlfriend* gives the readers to take hold of quintessence quickly as the writer remarks, "Once upon a time there was a Bihari boy called Madhav. He fell in love with a girl from Delhi called Riya. Madhav didn't speak English well. Riya did. Madhav wanted a relationship. Riya didn't. Riya just wanted a friendship. Madhav didn't. Riya suggested a compromise. She agreed to be his half girlfriend" (Bhagat *Half Girlfriend*).

On the success story of Bhagat's *Half Girlfried*, Dhiviya Hariharan rightly remarks "Once again Chetan Bhagat has beat his record of writing a book that can turn out the contents of your stomach by reading just few chapters". The New York Times cited Bhagat as "the biggest selling English language novelist in India's history". Bhagat writes on the common issues and adopts a realistic approach in his fictions with comic note leading to utter success. According to Iris Murdoch (1919-1999) "Fiction must contain comedy if it attains a realistic portrayal of human life" (Hague 9).

In *The Language of Humour*, Alison Ross (1949) remarks regarding the social aspect of comic elements and opines that perhaps the most important role of humor is to induce laughter. It reduces pain and lightens difficult situation. He defines humor as "something that makes a person laugh or smile" (1).

The novelist writes for the masses and most of times universal themes. F. Scott Fitzgerald (1996-1940) estimates humor as "...the part of beauty of all literature. You discover that your longings are universal longings, that you are not isolated from anyone. You belong". The novel begins as Chetan meets Madhav Jha, the protagonist of the novel in a room in Chanakya Hotel at Patna. Madhav initiates the story about a half girlfriend as dead leaving some journals behind. In a desperate mood the frustrated hero narrates the story. Madhav Jha, chief eccentric in the novel is six feet tall, black hair with intense looking eyes. In spite of poor grasp over English Madhav manages to score a seat in the prestigious English Medium St. Stephens College, New Delhi and falls in love with a high-class English-speaking rich Delhi girl, Riya Somani. Unlike Madhav she is super fluent in English. Chetan makes humor to bring out the stark reality of life which catches the attention of many youngsters in the society. Bhagat is adept in using this skill frequently to get our nerves relaxed. Like many of his novels Bhagat creates characters that go for searching identity. Chetan Bhagat was bit reluctant to give time to this Bihari boy. Bhagat calls Madhav up the next morning and hears the story about the difficulties entering St. Stephens College. Madhav faces problems because of bad English and gets admission through sports quota.

The strange title itself is humorous and allures the attention of the readers at first sight. It will make you laugh many times. In Indian society normally boys and girls are not clear about their relationship status with each other. On the other hand, an Indian youth may have wrong notions about girls. Most of the time the boy thinks that he is more than a friend with a girl, but the girl is still not girlfriend. Hence, a humorous title is assigned to the topic *Half Girlfriend*. The novelist very often tries to create laughter among the readers throughout the story. Madhav, an eager boy is trying hard convincing his favorite writer Chetan Bhagat to go through the journals of his presumed girlfriend. The writer gets a surprise look at the worst condition of multi folded journals as "many pages had holes, rats having snacked on them" (Bhagat 02).a

Being a poor English speaker, Madhav applies for admission into St. Stephen's College, New Delhi one of the famous colleges in India. On the interview day to get admission Madhav enquires about the location of interview room in strange English to a number of other applicants in the corridor. According to Madhav his English is not English, but 90% of Bihari Hindi with 10% bad English. Interestingly Madhav is turned to be an alien because of bad English when others mock at the protagonist and ask whether Madhav was there for the interview of peon. A sense of satire is smelt looking at the behavior of the guys and their comments as they mock at an innocent boy without a sense of compassion. Others present there ask "…are you interviewing for? peon?' the long-haired boy said and laughed". (08) An excellent sense of humor runs through the readers when Madhav faces the interview board and finds the three interviewer's grey hair which appears to him that the interviewers are not having smile since their hair turn grey. "The three old men sat in front of me. They looked like they had not smiled since their hair had turned grey" (09). Madhav with lot of difficulties had practiced to say good morning to the interviewers but faces troubles because one of the interviewers mentions that he has to greet all the three interviewers present there. 'Good morning, sir, sir and sir" (09).

In the process of interview Madhav gets ill smile and mockery from the interviewers as being a poor speaker in English. Bhagat satirizes the discouraging attitudes of the interviewers. Madhav confronts a number of obstacles during the interaction with the interviewers. He gets frustrated over the unwanted remarks by the interview board and interestingly all the three board members appear like 'English speaking monsters' to him. "Without these English-speaking monsters would eat me alive." The Bihari boy feels like cold drops of rain on scorching summer's day when Piyush Yadav, a sports teacher interacts with him in Hindi. Madhav feels really grateful to him and thinks like a homely condition with his presence who knows Hindi. 'You know Dumraon?' I said. I could kiss his feet." (Bhagat 10)

Another hilarious situation that binds the readers comes through the answer of Madhav on the question of selecting sociology as subject that makes Madhav hurdled to answer when the interviewers ask him "...you want to take sociology. Why? Prof. Fernandez said. 'It's an easy course, need to study. Is that it?' Prof. Gupta remarked" (11). In course of events Madhav has to give trials in the basketball court and on the performance of which will enable him get admission. Waiting for the turn Madhav had to consume time before the trial and smells a good gathering near girl's trial court that could attract audience easily. The novelist satirizes the audience's attitudes for nearing girls as he remarks that girls "... sports trials always garnered an audience" (14). Opportunity comes for Madhav to have a glance of a good-looking girl in the court and he feels something deep inside the heart towards the queen of the court who seeks a moment to talk to the girl. Anxiety reigns over him and he insists "to talk this girl at least once in your life" (15). Madhav observes Riya's game with keen interest and is satisfied over her playing in the court but hopes to change their point shooter. When the ball is overthrown outside the court and hits Madhav's head leading to dream the girl's vivacious beauty, he takes a moment to think on it that made Riya look in surprise. Riya's surprising look compels him to think about his dress code creates light moment for the readers.

> What?' she said. She surveyed me from top to bottom. I now wished I had worn better clothes. I had not changed out of my interview shirt and pants, both of which the tailor back home had stitched too close for me. I looked out of place on the basketball court. With my folder of certificates, I resembled a hero from those Hindi films of the seventies-the one who could not find a job (16).

Another comic aspect of the novel eases the readers when Madhav does not understand the English-speaking girl, Riya. Madhav gives some suggestion with an intention of improvement of their game. But the whistle blows for the second half of the game. Riya is compelled to leave and says to catch later. But the innocent chap does not get it, rather gets confused whether Riya is going to catch actually and perceives just opposite. Madhav gets baffled over various situations for the bad English and faces difficulties in expressing thoughts in English and lacks proper communication skill. The purpose of the writer is to create laughter among the readers and the objective is fulfilled through the central character of the novel. Piyush, the sports teacher in the middle of conversation points out at him saying a 'Bihari boy'. Madhav does not realise that Piyush has mentioned with a feeling of love and affection. Rather he considers it as an offence, and changes his mind dramatically and remarks-

> He could have taken offence. He had used the word 'Bihari' as if to say 'Watch, even this poor little Bihari can play', despite being a Bihari himself. However, he had helped me without knowing it, so I was grateful" (18).

At the very outset of the novel Madhav's heart goes round the tall and beautiful Riya and appreciates inside. Riya's perky voice startles most of times. Scanning over the name in the notice board to get admission in the college Madhav again comes in contact with Riya. It is hard to forget her even a single moment. Certain amount of intimacy develops between them. Both of them have conversation about their family. How Riya trusts in simplicity contrary to the family's stand. Her parents always indulge in hankering after money. With a proper tone of satire Bhagat aims at the intention of parents towards their children.

> Thanks. The problem is my family. They are obsessed with money. I'm not'. "I told them I want to study music after college. They want me to marry into some rich Marwari family and live like queen. I don't want to live like a queen. That is not what I dream of (32).

> Again, an experience of first kiss that came from an unintentional hit of Riya's forehead with Madhav's chin is really interesting and heart touching. Instead of feeling pain Madhav

feels happiness. Pain paled in front of joy the expressions by the novelist is quite amusing as,

> Riya's forehead hit my chin. I bit my tongue. "Hey she said not fair'. "I held my mouth in pain. Her forehead had hurt me badly. Steel the pain paled in comparison to the joy I felt from landing my first kiss (37).

After an unintentional hit with Riya's forehead, Madhav desperately considers that kiss to be a formal or natural kiss. In spite of having no response from Riya, Madhav is happy over the experience whose heart dances with happiness. In a humorous way the novelist mentions that the happiness felt from being selected to Bihar State Team comes to second position as replaced by the happiness of the kiss to Riya and the anxious chap considered "after kissing Riya, the selection day became the second happiest" (44). A girl's presence in a boy's hostel creates Ashu, Raman and Shailesh, friends of Madhav, feel uneasy or uncomfortable. Raman asks Madhav over the presence of a girl in the boy's hostel and confirms it that he "can steel smell the perfume,' Raman said and sniffed like a cartoon character, everyone laughed" (45).

Madhav's friends ask him questions whether Madhav loves Riya or not. In response to their questions Madhav thinks them asking stupid questions. 'Did I love her? Did the earth go round the sun? Did night follow day?' (Bhagat 46*)* Riya invites Madhav to her birthday party at Riya's village with family members. Madhav was bit frightened on his adjustment with a high-class people. At first Madhav meets the guard at Riya's residence on 100 Aurangazeb Road and thinks about their guard and tries to understand that the high-class people's layer of security that they avail. Madhav converses with the guard and smells a natural intimacy between two and considers that both of them belong to low class. "And you are Riya madams' friend? He said. I heard the condescension in his voice. A low class can smell another low-class" (49). In addition to humour Bhagat satirizes the gap between high- and low-class people in India. People from high class enjoy their life with abundance of wealth where the common men don't get even electricity.

> I entered the house, and found myself in a large living room with a shiny white marble floor. Glittering chandeliers hung from the fifteen-foot-high ceiling. Three sofa sets, upholstered in expensive silk were arranged in a U-shaped configuration. A teak and glass coffee table occupied the middle of the room. This is what real palace would look like if royals had actually money. I thought of my haveli with its peeling walls and cracked floors. Forget the chandeliers, we felt happy if we had less than five hours of power cuts (50).

Madhav finds Rohan, a rich boy having fancy accent, and gelled hair from London appears to be more intimate than Madhav. Madhav, a bit jealous of Rohan is baffled at the close behavior with Riya and doubts lest his boyfriend's seat be snatched by his rival. Rohan offers him drink. But to Madhav it is difficult and hardest time to digest. Rather Madhav prefers to "drink his blood" (57). Every time an impatient Madhav tries to bring his love before Riya and asks to be girlfriend. But contrary to the notion, Riya rejects the proposal and confesses to be a 'half girlfriend'. Madhav gets surprise to listen a term 'half girlfriend' and thinks about the hostel mates on this critical junction and wondered what she meant when she said 'half girlfriend'. Madhav necessitates the "expert panel" (68). Madhav was bit confused at the failed attempt to kiss Riya and asks his expert panel for an urgent meeting.

In response to the crisis Ashu, member to the expert panel counsels and consoles him and says that the concept of 'half' is not so bad and says, "Half is not bad. Depends on how you look at it; Ashu said'. Half-empty or half-full" (69). On the other hand, Shailesh, another member to the expert panel cautions him on the idea of making a high class, fluent English-speaking girl as girlfriend. Raman also supports him. Both of them make Madhav alert on the possibilities of cheating by Riya. The distinctive elements of humor and satire are quite visible through the description of the writer. The way the novelist uses the language relaxes burdened minds as, "Hell, it's more than a warning signs,' Sailesh said. It's a fire brigade siren on maximum volume using thousand-watt amplifiers. Don't you get it, Mr. Dumraon? She is playing with you" (69). Anyway the expert panel was also bit confused over the term 'half girlfriend'. No unanimous decision was taken by the panel. Rather in a comic way they advise Madhav to invite Riya to the boy's hostel room to change Riya and to convert the term half girlfriend to a full girlfriend and encourages him to make "Bihar proud..." (70). Riya on the other hand sticks to be just close friend, nothing more. Madhav gets breakup with Riya over the misunderstanding of girlfriend. The protagonist here feels guilty over sickness of male mentality. Eventually Riya gets her marriage proposal fixed with Rohan. Riya hands over a wedding invitation to Madhav ultimately making Madhav sink in desperation. The presumed girlfriend, the core of Madhav's heart giving a weeding card was hard to digest and he is saddened as a girl giving wedding card is basically like a giant "Game Over sign flashing in a video game" (88-89).

Another hilarious situation is created when Madhav considers that girls have the rights to hurt men. Madhav finds hard to breathe and considers the biscuit pocket inside the wedding card as a consolation prize and thinks deeply that, "Rohan gets Riya Madhav gets biscuits" (90). Moreover, in the story, Baghat depicts the real hostel life. Usually, hostellers get difficulties in filling their empty stomach. Madhav doesn't throw the biscuits and decides to stick to the golden rule of hostel not to throw food. Now the relation is cut off and Madhav somewhat repeats over his mistake hankering after a rich girl who had already left but at the same time repents over the downfall of personality. He tries to stick to a Bihari boy from Dumraon and says, "You belong to Dumraon in Bihar. That is who you are, Madhav Jha, I told myself, and that is all you will ever be and need to be" (94). Madhav feels disgusted at the rejection of Riya and doesn't accept the offer 'HSBC' job and returns home and consoles his mother to help in school administration. The school was facing a lot of financial crises. A true satirist is always conscious of the mistakes done by the institutions or the characters. "The true satirist is conscious of the frailty of institutions of man's devising and attempts through laughter not so much to tear them down as to inspire a remodeling" (William Thrall).

The author criticizes the condition of the village school due to inefficiency of fund which shows the real interest of the govt. on educational system of the country where fates are shaped for the interest of the nation. Madhav's mother confronts the hard consequences of the then condition of village school with various issues when she remarks as, 'every one eats my head' (95). The impression on the simple villagers by the elite class in the society is perfectly satirized in the words of the writer as, the "over-educated idiots in the big cities. Whenever they don't understand the villagers, they call them uneducated and old fashioned." (100) Madhav tries hard to help his mother in running the school. They get an opportunity from the local MLA to avail the lucky visit of Bill Gates, the richest person in the world and glimpse a bright chance to whitewash the pale looking walls of the school. Readers get a laughter ride for the language by the novelists as, 'Because of this white guy, my school will get a white wash" (119). With bit of hesitation Madhav accepts the offer from the US Delegation to give a speech in English, one which Madhav is afraid of. Interestingly Madhav practices his speech in front his mother as, "Good morning Mr.Bill Gates, Miss Samantha and guests. I Madhav welcoming you all to the Bihar. My school doing excellent coaching of childrens, farmers children, poor children, small children (...)I couldn't think of what to say next so as I referred to various kinds of children. I continued,. boy children, girl children, and many, many children" (125). Madhav faces a lot of difficulties in speaking the language and was compelled to think that "he has murdered English" all his life (134).

Miraculously Madhav discovers Riya Somani in a restaurant at Patna and avails the opportunity to look from her back and confirms none, but to be Riya. Unfortunately, Riya cannot notice Madhav and leaves. But Madhav is afraid of following Riya immediately lest she "might run away" (137). Incidentally Riya meets and offers a friendship to Madhav. Madhav is reluctant to go for just-friend deal again. But Riya distances from physical attachment. Riya is agreed to help in learning English speech to be delivered in the presence of Bill Gates. Everything goes well accordingly. But to utter surprise, Riya disappears from that occasion leaving a letter to Madhav that she is caught with lung cancer and death is inevitable.

The author attacks the attitude of Madhav's mother who doesn't accept Riya, a divorcee as daughter-in-law. She is unresponsive to the happiness of her son. Now Madhav is in New York and is informed about an Indian singer's performance at the night bar. To the heart-breaking surprise of the readers Madhav discovers Riya Somani there. To our utter delight two hearts are united with deep and heart-breaking emotion. The novel comes to an end with a rosy picture of their conjugal life at Dumraon. Riya's presence made Madhav's life colorful and they now lead happy life with their son. "Comedy is the art of making people laugh without making them puke" (Steve Martin)

Humour is the important aspect of everyday life. The point is that this tool can be used to face the hardest times in our life and at the same time we can appreciate some of the most outstanding times. With a pinch of humour we can change our life to a different direction however we are over shadowed by the shadows of sadness. In fact, it is true that without humor hard times seem harder to handle. Jane Austen in her *Pride and Prejudice*, Mark Taiwan in his *The Adventures of Huckelberry Finn*, Harper Lee in her novel *To Kill a Mockingbird* and Charles Dicken in his *Great expectations* have wide impact and lasting impressions on the readers. Throughout the novel Chetan Bhagat has been successful in using tremendous skill of humor and satire. Indianness in his themes makes his novels more interesting who invented the genre of contemporary Indian writing. Before these average Indian readers were fed a diet of Sydney Sheldon, Jeffrey Archer, and John Grisham etc. all of whom wrote about American system. Indian authors Shobha De, R.K.Narayan, Amitav Ghosh and others choice of setting were in a long bygone era or just too outside the scope of common man's dreams. But Chetan Bhagat's novels are directed to the common man's dreams. He beautifully presents a common tale of common man of India. In fact, he takes up issues which reverberate with the masses. The novel is entertaining. Bhagat ensures reader's engagement for the most part of the book and there is simple humor peppered throughout the story with ample entertainment and that holds mass appeals. After all it's a charming love story that provides a lot of humor and satire to the readers. By means of good humor we can have opportunity to step back and see what is most important in life. To cut the long story short it is true that Chetan Bhagat has shaped the many Indian's reading habits creating light moments for readers. Because of the funny elements his novels are not for the elite and limited readership but for the masses.

11

Sharp Reflection of Maladies that Afflict Indian Society at Various Levels: An Analysis of Chetan Bhagat's *2 States: The Story of My Marriage*

The world of fiction in contemporary Indian English literature is incomplete without the contribution of Chetan Bhagat. Being an immortal name in this field; he has acclaimed a wide reputation among the youth and has enriched the Indian literature with appropriate use of humor and satire through his fictions. It is rightly observed that he is on the rise among the younger generation and has reserved space in the core of their hearts. As he is considered the biggest selling Indian novelist in India's history, some extent of criticism is obviously expected. In his novels every aspect related to life and society i.e. Problems, hopes and aspirations of the youth, love, sex and marriage have been reflected through appropriate use of humor and satire. In '*2 States*: *The Story of my Marriage,* a fictional version of love story, Bhagat has tried his best level to raise his voice against so called traditional and orthodox views on marriage. It's an awesome journey from a rasgulla friendship to a buffet dinner. In true sense Bhagat has revolutionized the ideas against the malady lingering and deep seated in the Indian society and that afflict the society at various levels of life and living in terms of comic mode of burlesque and satire.

Bhagat's *2 States-The Story of My marriage* is an autobiographical love story of the writer in which two love birds from two states of India, namely Ananya Swaminathan (his wife

Anusha) a Tamil girl and Krish Malhotra (Chetan Bhagat) a Punjabi boy. The fiction is a lovely, heart-touching and attractive literary masterpiece in contemporary Indian literature. The story starts from IIT Ahmedabad where the two love birds come in contact with each other. Being the prettiest and attractive girl in the campus Ananya remains in the hearts of most of the IITians. Eventually both Krish and vivacious Ananya come in close contact and spend many evenings together for study and fell in deep love although they are from two opposite cultural communities. The life of these two protagonists appears great for them until their family meet each other. In spite of their romantic attachment and seer longing to lead a conjugal life thing do not happen to their expectation. In fact, the readers are entertained by the incredible humor ingrained in this part of the novel. Both of them had to convince their orthodox family. Krish, a determined boy to get his love finally got it. The story is in perfect humorous tone that intends at easing pain and creates laughter among the readers with an appropriate use of satire.

The major portion of the fiction is depicted about The Punjabi and Tamil culture and the pride and prejudices for each other. Parson in his claims that "culture... consists in those patterns relative to behavior and the products of human action which may be inherited, that passed on from one generation to generation independently of the biological genes" (8). Again, according to Hofstede "culture is the collective programming of the mind which distinguishes the members from one category of people from the other"(51).The story is based on the cultural clashes that tries to stick to own identity.

The author needs appreciation for the dominating humor throughout the fiction. The novel is a romantic journey of a culturally opposite cultures. Both of them meet each other over the quarrel of Ananya with the adamant mess worker on the issues of disgusting breakfast. Eventually the matter is interfered by Krish when he realizes to lessen the intensity of quarrel by offering his own rasgulla to the prettiest girl and feels that sacrificing own rasgulla may go to be useless and brings no fruit to him. Young

Krish languishes and repents over losing his own for nothing. A good sense of humor provides laughter ride to the readers. "Give mine to her' (...)'she'll never date you; it is a rasgulla down the drain. I scolded myself" (05).

Dreams and passion dominate and hunt the characters. Krish dreams of Ananya and her never ending beauty and repents over losing and wasting time in conversing with her with no advance in love. A just friend deal doesn't satisfy the indomitable instincts. Krish's thoughts over the usability and profit of conversation create a sense of humor. The protagonist considers himself as a victim and regrets that "Why would any guy want to be only friends with a girl? It's like a agreeing to be near a chocolate cake and never eat it. It's like a sitting in a racing car but not driving it?" (09). Ankur and Aditya, two other characters who had already proposed Ananya never consider the embarrassment over their rejection. They don't take it seriously adding to another comic description. After being rejected they sit the whole session with the rejecter; careless to their dismissal.

More over through perfect use of satire Bhagat attacks the educational system of the nation when Prof. Chatterjee, a two – decade veteran gives a sinister smile over the answer of an inquisitive girl in the class that doesn't suit to the ethics of his profession. It's the clear indication of the deteriorating and faulty educational system of our country. "Notice, class, notice. This is the state of economics education in the country. Top graduates don't know the basics. And then they ask –why is India backward?" (10-11) With an intention of advancing intimacy or contact with Ananya Krish gives a proposal of studying together but at the same time tries to hide his inner instinct and pretends to be that he never wants to be included in the list of her proposers and says, "Hey, I have no interest in being number eleven. This is purely for study reason" (12).

The novel again catches the attention of the readers when Bhagat satirizes the womanly tendency of deep attraction towards jewelry that happened to the members of Ananya. "All old women wore as much gold as their body could carry" (Bhagat14). A comic comparison is made again when Krish compares Ananya's parents in a strange way that they look scary and wonders that how can these scary looking parents create so cute? Of course, Chetan Bhagat with a blend of humour and wit has motivated many young minds. Bhagat's words and the skill of using them at right time create a lot of light moments for the readers when he remarks in the fiction, "How can such scary looking parents create something so cute?" (14)

When the two love birds want to fly high plenty of remarks pour in on the developing intimacy between Ananya and Krish as a vivid example of Bhagat's skill of satirizing the Indian youth of giving their valuable time and giving unnecessary remarks on others. Writers, like Bhagat, has tried to touch the real life condition of the youth in hostel where Krish is bit reluctant to maintain aesthetic appeal that represents the carelessness of educated youth. "Unlike her room, there was no aesthetic appeal to mine. I had left the red bricks bare, and they looked like prison walls. My originally white bed sheet had turned grey after being washed in acid in the IIT hostels. My desk had only books, unlike Ananya who always had cut flowers from campus lawns or arty incense holders or other objects that men never put on their shopping lists" (23).

The eager readers again glimpse a taste of humor through the appreciation of moles that are below the lower lip of Ananya. The moles are just fifty percent market share in the mind space of Krish who had appeals to the sensuous beauty of Ananya. Bhagat remarks that the mole may be tiny but "...but it at least has a fifty percent market share in terms of mind space" (24).

At present the Indian youths are on the cross roads of building their career and reaching at their destination. In this context Krish is in search of getting a job that suits to his interests. Bhagat was eager to join in CITI BANK, the most important bank in India who is at the critical juncture and turmoil of life. At the interview Krish answers the interviewers in a comic way. "Finally, they asked a big question. "Why Citi bank? "I want Citi Bank because none of the other five banks worked out, I sucked in my breath along with my stupid thoughts.BS time buddy, I thought, the ten seconds that will determine your career start now" (35). In fact, Bhagat has left no stone unturned to express humor and satire throughout the novel related to the issues of the youth. Bhagat's hero is really bored on 'just-friend' deal with Ananya. Krish thinks that "Why should any guy want to be only friends with a girl? It's like agreeing to be near a chocolate cake and never it. It's like sitting in a racing car and not driving it?" (09)

The heart-breaking story moves on. Both of Krish and Ananya get their job suited to them respectably. To get their dreams materialized they have tried their best and convinced their parents to introduce each other's parents and set Goa as the destination but reaches at a sour note of relationship between Krish's mom and Ananya's parents. Here Bhagat, with a mixture of wit and humor satires at the orthodox and so-called traditional views of both parents towards their children. They are in fact more interested on their own happiness rather than the happiness in their children. In the words of Bhagat "From biscuits to brides, if there is anything that their children really want, parents have a problem, I said" (39).

The novelist tries to attack the conservative traditions of the society through his characters. The readers are better connected with the characters and feel like their own life situation is being described. The writer uses perfect satire delivering a message to all. In a pleasant surprise Krish finds a job in Chennai, the home town of Ananya and aims to ease and smooth the relationship with Ananya's parents. Chetan's humor dances in full force in the hearts of the readers as he talks about various aspects of Tamilian living; gets puzzling. Krish finds it curious that how every Tamilian wants to be up at the break of the very early morning and compares of sparse, functional homes of Tamils to ostentatious homes of the Punjabis.

At his workplace Bhagat finds certain element of sycophancy in his boss named Bala; which is even found in the Tamil community. The novelist satirizes at the financial management of corporate bank. In true sense the author's desire for humor make his books hugely readable.

The novel again comes to the final section when Krish goes through a low morale over motivating his parents for their marriage. After a number of attempts by both Krish and Ananya they have come to be successful with a lot of hurdles and struggling. Krish's boisterous family come to join the marriage at Chennai and are stunned that that they have to be ready at the dawn contrary to their idea which makes them that the rituals are generally funny. Bhagat writes that "It's a marriage or torture" (247). Bhagat did a fantastic job of introducing the readers to the both characters are from two different states and two opposing cultures get mingled to indicate the oneness of India. Apart from this the novel is typical in the reality of Indian society that it is how important to get the families approval before marriage. The back cover page gives a glance the readers:

> "Boy loves girl. Girl loves boy. They get married.
> In India, there are a few more steps:
> Boy loves girl. Girl loves boy.
> Girl's family has to love boy's family. Boys' family has to love girl's family.
> Girl and boy still love each other. They get married."

Generally, parents look at their own interest. With a good sense of humor and comic vision, Bhagat has brought the audience to see the Punjabis and Tamils get connected. In the words of Bhagat it is an attainment of the greater purpose of uniting Indians from different parts of our nation and says, "Only for the sake of uniting the nation" (267). "The novel is excellent because it conveys how youngistan fights oldistan to get the approval for marriage". The story keeps the readers related with characters. The language is subtle, readable, interesting and all hilarious. Bhagat's technique of binding the young readers is quite lovable. More over the patriotic approach brings the oneness among the Indians.

Contemporary Indian Youth Caught between Cultures

Bhagat's *Two States: The Story of My Marriage* is a sequel to his debut novel *Five Point Someone* in which the protagonist Krish an IIT graduate and Ananya a graduate in economics is caught between two different cultures. The novel depicts some dark area of the society of cultural differences. The fiction presents more independent and matured youths in the name of Krish and Ananya. Both of them coming from different background and cultures create trouble for their union. Bhagat satirizes the traditional views and opinions of their parents in connection of their children's happiness. The novel beautifully presents the true picture of Indian cultures, ideologies, complexities and orthodox feelings prevalent in our society. The theme of the novel establishes synthesis between inner life and outer social reality. It tries to reflect that culture of a particular society is always determinant of one's identification. The novel is a representation of contemporary youth's changing needs in a first changing society. The present youth no more prefer to the dominance of patriarchal and matriarchal system of the society which has been observed in previous literature. Their dependence on parental guidance or whoever is the boss in the family starts to lose ground in the changing time. The fact can't be minimized that factors like western culture and rapid advancement of science and technology necessitated the beginning of new system.

In fact, the new trend as the impact of modern education changed the outlook of Indian youth. Today's youth started to redefine their needs on the basis of their compatibility and individual needs. Bhagat deals such issues in his novels where he wants to invite a new approach to youth of contemporary India. His 2 States is a beautiful depiction of contemporary youth caught between cultures against their individual necessities and choices.

The present fiction is a manifestation of contemporary youth's changing needs in a changing society. The old concept of 'youth' is changed. Previously it was considered as a docile and inhibited which is replaced by self-dependence and freedom in this 21st century. His aspirations are distinctively marked by his instincts; Guidance is subject to decline. It is amazingly visible that influence of western culture and tradition has its noticeable impact among

the Indian youths. But the clash between the old culture and the new is rampant in current novel. The age-old traditional system confronts with the new being influenced by globalization and individualism. There is a wide gap between the generations that affects the growth or progress.

The novel narrates the two different cultures and their differences making a huge and mountainous problem in front of Krish and Ananaya. In fact, their relationship gets obstruction and they lost academic progress. Probability of better vocation to their expectation is no more present. Ananya Swaminathan is a typical Brahmin, modern in her approach to life, attitudes and dressing. She maintains a balance but faces a lot of problems because of cultural differences. Coming from IIMA they fell in love and prefer to maintain their self-chosen life style. They didn't want to disclose their relationship at the initial stage in the campus lest the cultural gap create hindrance. Their consistency in relationship and intimacy brings them togetherness even at Ananya's dormitory. Gradual development in their relationship came to the notice of their parents. Just now the problem starts. Inter-caste marriage is still a taboo in India. Love knows no boundary. It blossoms through the suitability of the love birds. But the Indian perspectives in this regard seem insurmountable. Parents must understand the feelings of their children and should give justice. Bhagat's minute observation of the campus life is linked to the different cultural setting. The eager boy wants his love but faces a lot of problems due to cultural differences. India is a country of diversity leading to various issues. In fact we have to resolve them at our best which doesn't happen initially.

Racial discrimination is prevalent in this fiction when the anxious parents look for perfect matches for their children. In fact, we are outwardly modern but inwardly we still live in past. The novel is set on the background of 'North-South-Division' highlighting the cultural diversities. The author exposes the backwardness among Indians to accept the inevitable changes and criticizes the non-acceptance of inter-caste marriage which is still considered as a social stigma.

The differences between the generations concerning the different ideologies never want to bring a compromise in the process of smooth relationship. The conversation between Krish, his mother and Shipra Massi reflect a wide gap between two cultures related to ethnicity or race. Shipra Massi says, "Son ... that is all fine. But how can we marry Madrassi? Tomorrow your cousin will want to marry a Gujurati" (Bhagat 69). The middle part of the novel narrates about the couple's important episodes of struggling to conquer the hearts of the two families.

The most important aspect of Bhagat's novel is to strike out that how the characters negotiate two clamoring cultures. Ananya's parents are more conservative and orthodox to approve the relationship. Among the Tamil Brahmins the autonomy of children is less. On the other hand, Krish's growth in a Punjabi family is largely influenced by all the relatives around her. The novelist criticizes the feelings of the parents towards their children's happiness. At last, they got united but not without serious and hectic confrontations from both families.

In fact, Bhagat narrates the story about some critical issues in a light way so that it attracts others. Definitely the novel gives a cultural shock wit reference of various sensitive issues of the orthodox society. Bhagat bears an opinion that love knows no boundaries. No caste, creed, religion, states or country take position before true love. This wonderful aspect of life triumphs over the rest. Nowadays diversity is typical in most of workplaces. Globalized world with advancement of technology the world has been shortened and the novelist necessitates meeting the challenge of cultural barriers.

After all it's a novel of lot of laugh and light moments for the readers which are loosely based on the life of Bhagat's own life. On the other hand, it's the story of many young Indians who are in the critical cross roads in their love matter, facing troubles from their parents or the society. Major characters are college goers. The novel has humor as an undercurrent and its black humor. In fact Bhagat is being criticized that he writes the issues that appeal to the masses and writes very light subjects. It's hard to minimize the scale of his reputation in Indian literature. Rather he doesn't make it esoteric which might perhaps alienate the readers from him. The novel got emotions, sex, friendship, music, betrayal and exploitation in a comic and satiric way. The book is humorous taking a dig at both the Punjabi and Tamil community. Common people can connect to the Indian sentiments that are beautifully portrayed throughout the novel. Bhagat tries to maintain humor consistently. All most all of his novels go round the life of youth and issues related. In fact, he depicts their real-life pictures and entertains all classes and cadres of people.

The book is written in simple style and laymen's language that creates much laughter among the readers. The novel touches the theme of intensity of love through educated and intelligent youths, it touches the issues of intense relationship predicaments, it touches the problems related to dowry and again it touches the egos and eagerness. The novel reflects the crisis of relationship and crisis of social identity. It talks about that how genuine love can minimize the gap between differences and detachment. He manages to retain his sense of humor relating to the harsh realities of life. He can feel the pulse of the nation and narrates it almost in a comic way attracting a huge reading mass. He is apt in depicting the social and other topical issues in a perfect comic and satiric way of description. The magnitude of such great thoughts is really magnified.

Since the inception of Indian literature in English it is very much evident that today's status is an outcome of gradual development through the ages. English language and literature came to India with the colonizers as a beautiful gift. It did the job of various areas like education, communication and literary effort. Hence English language and literature in India put its mark with the arrival of east India Company. English spread its impact throughout this vast land by and by. Educationists, political thinkers and the social elites adopted the language for convenience of communication or interaction paving the way for the rest in the society. Thus, English language gained its ground in India and

English literature is the byproduct of it. Indian English literature originated as a result of the beginning of English education in India under colonial rule. In current years it has attracted far-reaching attention both in India and abroad. Indian English Literature has attained maturity with the passage of time. Initially all other forms of literature like poetry, drama and non-fiction writings were impressive to the masses. During the initial period of writing the premier kind was poetry. It was followed by other kinds of literature especially drama. Fiction was actually last to arrive as this form far exceeded to other forms of literature.

Initially socio-cultural, economic and political upheavals in the nation had a great impact on Indian English fiction. But gradually fiction became the manifestation of the most powerful and consciousness of life and society. Its journey to the present day witnessed a rapid change and fiction got its due status perhaps during the last decades. Today Indian English fiction reached at the apex even in the realm of world literature. The realm of today's fiction is gardened and nurtured by a number of writers. The novelists undertaken in this thesis belong to the contemporary Indian English who are distinguished from others in their use of humor and satire to ease the mind of the readers in particular and to rectifying the society as a whole. As a colonial child Indian novel paved the way for the next generation of the writers. Contemporary writers have wide impressions on the readers not only in India but have a great impact on the world readers.

Fiction is the most dominant form of literary expressions and today it has been able to acquire a prestigious position in Indian English literature. In fact, it is unanimous across the world that fiction is the most influential literary form of for the exploration of experiences and ideas in the context of our time. Prof. M.K.Naik rightly remarks, "One of the most notable gifts of English education to India is prose fiction for though India was probably a fountain head of storytelling, the novel as we know was an important form of west".

The fictional creations up to the ninetieth century were written by writers who belong to the presidencies of Bengal and Madras. As mentioned above the Indian English fiction came into existence only in the later part of the twentieth century most of them were emotionally attached with their regional languages. They considered that English was a foreign language but the concept gradually changed. The writers started to believe that learning English is not a slave mentality. People started using it for speeches, articles, pamphlets and discussing several current problems. Pramod Kumar Singh says, "In the mid ninetieth century, Raja Ramomohan Roy had initiated social programmers and, in the process, he favored English language or spreading the wealth of information and culture available in British publication". An advocacy of social reform was a significant idea in the writings of early fiction. Place of women in the society, suffering of the peasants and the decaying upper classes got importance among the initial writers.

The Gandhian whirlwind blew across the country during 1920 to 1927.Mahatma Gandhi was the core of influence among the writers. Under his dynamic leadership new ideas and notions got pace. The nationwide movement of Gandhi not only influenced the common man of the country but also the themes of the novels. The impact was quite remarkable and exemplary. It can be perceived by the works of many authors with the burning issues by that time.

The Indian English fiction got ripeness and wide applause in the post-independence era. After the achievement of independence, the novels experienced a change in themes. There was conceptual shifting in writing. Individualism started to take the source instead of public issues. The feelings of sticky situation, fretfulness, isolation, disappointment and aloofness became the major issues which were best expressed through humor and satirical expressions. Besides some other themes like fantasy, humor started to get prominence in the process. Degradation of moral values, impact of westernization, dysfunctional bureaucratic attitudes, nausea, cultural differences, blind belief and superstitions of rural India and the stark reality of the society and life are observed in the writings of post-independence era. The emergence of the 'big three' was a greatest landmark in the journey of fiction writing to the present-day status. The writings of these three novelists took the right direction of the fiction writings in India. In fact, the Indian novel got its identity because of them. They defined the vicinity in which Indian novel was to function.

During latter half of the twentieth century yet another class of Indian fiction writers came into existence with variety of themes and issues in literature. Novelists like Salman Rushdie, Vikram Seth, Upamanyu Chatterjee, Allan Seally, Sashi Despande, Namita Gokhle, Sashi Tharoor, Farukh Dhondi, Amitav Ghosh etc. contributed well to Indian English fiction.

Although there is no water tight compartments separating contemporary writers from others still Indian contemporary literature is gigantic in its range and encompasses literature of various genres and style. Although impact of western philosophy and content was visible in Indian literature still Indian writers are well enough to maintain their uniqueness in writing with Indian flavor and richness. Use of humor and satire got prominence in some of the contemporary writers. Although it will be repetition of mentioning the same it is better to cite for recapitulation as the dissertation examines the role of humor and satire in the contemporary Indian English fiction.

Literature mirrors the society. On the other hand, it is considered as a reflection of good values in the society and intends to rectify it. Most of the writers try their best level to criticize their societies depicting people's life and situations. Language is the vehicle to transform the bad one to good. The purpose of the writer is meant for that. At the same time they aim at to create laughter and ease the pain of the people in society. Writers of all ages respond to this trend. Hence the use of humor and satire is inevitable to discuss.

Humor and satire are closely related, but there are certain distinctions between them. As a form of criticism satire uses humor to accomplish its goals. Humor is the propensity of particular cognitive experiences to rouse laughter and present entertainment.

The term takes its origin from ancient Greek which primarily meant to control human health and emotion. It is the quality of action, speech or writing which excites amusement. Being amused makes one to feel good. We expect literature to do more than simply amusement. True purpose of literature is elevating our spirits. It is the ability to others laugh and make him burden free. Moreover, it is the most effective device which is used to please the readers. It serves many functions in literature. The functions of humour are varied and many. Steve Martin rightly remarks, "Comedy is the art of making people laugh without making them puke". From the functional perspectives of humor, it is considered that besides the primary function of humor providing amusement or entertainment to the readers it also develops social relationship in the society. It reduces social distances through interactions and facilitates interpersonal relations.

Jean Weis Gerber defines satire as a genre of literature, irony is the reasoning rhetorical tool; humor is substance. Satire is described as a literary art of diminishing and a literary art with a corrective purpose of diminishing or derogating a subject by making it ridiculous. Satire can evoke the attitude of amusement, contempt, scorn or resentment for the betterment of society and exposes people's stupidity and vices in the context of contemporary or topical issues. It is a genre of literature which targets to mend idiocy, vices, follies, abuses and shortcomings among the individuals, corporations, govt. or society into improvement. Its greater purpose is always constructive to bring changes in a positive manner. Novel as the form of literature very often employs humor and satire as a weapon to reach at the huge number of readers. According to Irish Murdoch "Fiction must contain comedy if it attains a realistic portrayal of human life" As fiction mirrors the life the literary form has been well used by many writers to expound the lighter side and hideous things of our life. The purpose of comic vision is to satirize a given circumstance which the world literature has witnessed a lot.

In contemporary Indian English fiction, Upamanyu Chatterjee, Anurag Mathur and Chetan Bhagat are three distinguished creative writers who use humor and satire to make light of serious and often taboo subjects sometimes generating discomfort ,serious thoughts as well as amusement to the audience .Each of these novelists stands out for this uniqueness but all three of them have adopted common narrative techniques of employment of humor and satire in decoding the complicate ,multiple existences of an individual in a postmodern era. While Upamanyu Chatterjee's novels are predominantly informed by scathing satire against Indian bureaucracy and moral depravity, the novels of Anurag Mathur are comic portrayals of the power-hungry politicians and the pseudo elite ways of the idolizing the west. Chetan Bhagat's novels are on the other hand are a sharp reflection of the maladies that afflict Indian society at various levels of life and living in terms of the comic mode of burlesque and satire.

In the realm of contemporary Indian English fiction Anurag Mathur, Upamanyu Chatterjee and Chetan Bhagat deserve wide acclamation for their valuable contribution related to use of humor and satire in their novels. All three of them tried to their best level to reach at the huge number of readers making many light moments and easing pain and suffering from their mind. At the same time, they intend to attack the superstitions, blind believes orthodox attitudes of the society. The trio have been successful in appropriating the use of humor and satire with an intention of articulating the irrationality of traditional beliefs and superstitions of rural India, the aspirations of the middle class to attain the life of prosperity and comfort, the neo-colonial attitude of exploitation of the poor and innocent Indians by those who appropriate power through corrupt and devious means, the grotesque ways of imitating western life styles and manners and self-seeking mindset of politicians bureaucrats and businessman.

Anurag Mathur's *Making the Minister Smile* published in 1996, is a humorous fiction on an American coming to India and at the same time a critic on the Indian way of life. It gives a picture of Indian poverty, politics and eccentricities from foreigner's point of view. The fiction is a presentation of the relationship between Indian politicians and the businessman. As a novel of social realism, it is full of humor, laughter, wit and surprises with packed of social satire. Corruption and the evil nexus in the Indian way of life and political circles got attracted. The novel exposes the controversy surrounding a company and its workers union. The controversy goes on between the union leaders and that management but fail to come to an amicable solution to resolve the factory problem makes the crux of the story. The author has been successful to maintain the wry sense of humor.

Anurag Mathur's Inscrutable American is a dash of spice, mixed with humor, seasoned with suspense and toasted with a glass of drama. The novel gives a completely humorous take. The story narrates the experiences of an Indian boy named Gopal in a small university campus in U.S.A. who hails from Jajau, a small town of Madhya Pradesh. The whole story is comic and hilarious which centers round Gopal in America and America with Gopal. Gopal's one year spent in America and his English provides a lot of amusement to the readers. Mathur differentiates America to India through a fictitious character and brings out issues of racial discrimination and sexual abuse in the country. Gopal's mysterious notion on Americans, his simplest attitude in every step of intimacy and the language he uses gives a plenty of amusement to the audience. The readers get acquainted with the characters and situations easily. As far as humor quotient is concerned Anurag Mathur tries to make the most of the situations in his fifth novel 'The Country is going to the Dogs'. It is light hearted in its tone and seeks to attain its objective to create laughter among the readers from its very outset. Published in 2014 the novel attracts a huge number of students and seems a humorous novel with a great deal of satire. It's a critique on the Indian mindset of modernism and conservatism. Three years of experience in the United States helped Mathur to come up with a theme of cultural conflict between two societies which according to him is the class conflict between our conventional traditional upbringing and the new India. Mathur's novels aim at corrective measures and the humor is subtly integrated.

The world of Upamanyu Chatterjee's novels is basically based on the satiric elements which have been detailed through alienation, regression and post-colonial hangover of the late twentieth century adolescences and youth of India. His novels are the depictions of realistic social conditions of the time. Upamnyu Chatterjee is one of the important voices in the domain of Indian novel in English literature that has profound and comic vision and lasting impression on the readers. Chatterjee always tries to depict the comic aspects of everyday life. Various forms of comedy like farce, satire and irony got prominence. The maturation of his characters is characterized by a large number of social, historical, political and filial accumulations to be reflected in individual subjectivity through proper sense of humor and satire. The absence of struggle to construct identity is a very conspicuous motif in the novels. Characters become victims of pitfalls and ditches obstructing comfortable assertion of their existence.

English, August: An Indian Story is well written and refreshingly witty and comical. The marvelous aspect of this novel is use of humor. The story revolves round a westernized city boy who is marooned in a small village with a job he is not interested in at all. Western influence on young generation and huge difference between urban and rural lives is also another theme which is beautifully described. It's a witty commentary on the mammoth apparatus on the Indian bureaucracy with its inefficient administrative officers. Again, the novel is the representation of alienated and misled youth of contemporary India which is severely satirized by the novelist. The life of the protagonist is largely shadowed by the pull between the ethos's of modernity and tradition. It is again fueled by the fondness of the colonial desire and individual necessity. The characters attempt to assert their identities become illusion by the evils of the society. More the characters try to search the right path more the problem they face under the socio-political temporalities of the period. Agastya's story is realistic, enjoyable, moving and timeless that merits a great compliment for funniest elements enriched with. Most of the characters actually lead a life of duality-one in superficially abstract plank and another in psychological inner realities. The readers can witness their false being. This is one of the funniest books of the writer and perhaps the best effort at comic and satiric blend of mind. It is a thought-provoking ride of the Indian bureaucracy and its many unwanted evils through the eyes of considerate and skeptical individual named Agastya, the protagonist of the novel. In fact, the book is a funny critique on the feelings of alienation, dislocation, daily musings and deep and confusing thoughts of Agastya. Marijuana and excessive alcohol prevent Agastya from confusion or perplexity. The author tries to expose various follies and vices through the character of Agastya and in the process provides hilarious moments for the readers. The author has made references to Indian objects. Humor is obviously the main stay of the novel. The humor in this novel ranges from amusing to the stupid, from the ridiculous to satire. The flow of comic reference is spontaneous and unhindered. Chatterjee manages to take situation of enormous variety of Indian mindsets and vices. The novel helps the readers to discover the new areas of vices and follies in the way Agastya looks at the world and is remarkable that readers like the protagonist in spite of all his misdoings and confusion over it. In spite of misdoings readers like because Agastya possesses lack of self-importance and self-confidence. Agastya manages to endear himself to the readers. The novelist is more satirical giving a reference to the Indian bureaucrats who are same and unchanged in spite of all the rules provided to them. The book is truly unique and the great idea is well executed.

Chetan Bhagat is one of the most well-known authors in the landscape of Indian English fiction in recent times. Known as a, columnist, script writer, motivational speaker and a youth icon, Bhagat has penned down novels that have tested tremendous popularity and success among Indian audiences. Born in Delhi in a middle-class Punjabi family, Bhagat did most of his education in the national capital. The critical and the theoretical discourse on Chetan Bhagat's status as a fiction writer writing in English and the popularity, he has acquired in couple of years has made him a legendary figure and the best seller English language author all over the world. In all of his fictions he touches the sentiments of youths and provides the light moments for the youths. In fact, Bhagat is one of the leading novelists of this school of fiction writing in India. Again, the global scientific wisdom and traditional Indian culture have placed Indian youth as a cross-road; he is a challenging task of balancing conflicting traits. Bhagat comes out with his writing tales about modern India; the ethos and isolation of an entire generation and an undercurrent of humanity. Bhagat uses humor to bring out the stark reality in the lives of educated youths, their human concern and their struggles and dilemmas. His '2 States: The Story of My Marriage' projects the true spirit of nationalism which is based on two main characters of Ananya Swaminathan and Krish Malhotra through perfect use of humor and satire that creates much laughter among the readers. Bhagat's *Half Girlfriend* reflects the stark reality of Indian youth.

As it is difficult to include all his novels from the perspectives of satiric and humorous elements, efforts have been made to go through his two novels i.e. *Two States: The Story of My Marriage* and *Half Girlfriend.* The element of humor is predominant in all his novels. Bhagat's novels have humor as an undercurrent and it is black humor which is considers that suffering as ridiculous rather than deplorable, or it considers that human existence is satirical and pointless but somehow comic. On the other hand, it is called black humor that uses farce and low comedy to make clear that individuals are helpless fatalities of destiny and character. Bhagat makes his humor to depict the contemporary society in a realistic approach.

His "2 States-The story of My marriage" is an autobiographical love story of the writer in which two love birds from two states of India, namely Ananya Swaminathan (his wife Anusha) a Tamil girl and Krish Malhotra (Chetan Bhagat) a Punjabi boy, were in deep love. It is a lovely, heart-touching and attractive literary masterpiece in contemporary Indian literature. The story starts from IIT Ahmedabad where two came in contact with each other. Being the prettiest and attractive girl in the campus Ananya remains in the hearts most of the IITians. But eventually both Krish and vivacious Ananya came in close contact and spent many evenings together for study and fell in deep love although they are from two opposite cultural communities. The life of these two protagonists appears great for them until their family meet each other. In spite of their romantic attachment and seer longing to lead a conjugal life thing do not happen to their expectation. In fact, the readers are entertained by the incredible humor ingrained in this part of the novel. Both of them had to convince their orthodox family. Krish, a determined boy to get his love finally got it. The story is narrated in perfect humorous tone that intends at easing pain and creates laughter among the readers with an appropriate use of satire.

The humor in this novel is mostly situational. The cultural difference between the love birds where Krish is a Punjabi from Delhi while Ananya a Tamil Brahmin becomes the springboard for many humorous references and comic situations. Most of situations Chetan Bhagat uses humor to deal serious issues in light manner and make his readers to feel ease even in difficult time. His fictional pieces of writing have restored him remarkable success and this would not be exaggeration if we consider his success because of his light moments or situations created in his writings.

The very story of the novel reveals an important factor concerning Bhagat's writing simple style and the selection of subject matter. He has raised the fundamental issues of love affair in Indian middle-class family. Though it is a fictitious work it touches the youth sentiments of Indian middle-class society. With perfect satiric intention he realistically presents the life and dilemma of Indian youth falling in love coming from different religious and cultural background. Indian youth have to struggle against the so-called norms of the society to get the approval of their parents before marriage. In spite of their willingness both of their parents have to give consent. It is a herculean task to motivate both sides that creates lot of trouble for them. Bhagat hits at the cultural extremism and satires at the attitude of society towards the happiness of their children.

In the present novel, Bhagat has tried to attack at the cultural confrontation before the future of their children. He warns that how the evils of the society give great shock on the behavioral aspects of its members. He shows that inter caste marriage and cultural differences create lot of problems and even the parents don't allow this type of marriage. Sometimes the boy and the girl suffer from enormous mental and emotional ordeal and they even commit suicide making a great loss to the society. The very title of the novel is a reminiscent of the peculiar cultural distinctiveness of the north and the south. This confrontation is illustrated within a lively touch of humour. He evokes a comic situation when Krish's mother makes racial and sarcastic remarks on Ananya's family. Bhagat exposes the orthodox attitude of Indian middle-class culture. Racial discrimination got satirized through his perfect use of satire.

As a sincere and avid advocate of national integrity Chetan Bhagat tries to criticize the evils of the society and suggests avoiding the issue of racism and considers being a national threat. Regarding the use of language Chetan Bhagat is undisturbed at the criticism and considers shattering such kind of criticism. He doesn't like verbosity rather prefers to use common man's language which is understood by many. By using the language of the younger generation, he comes to be closer to the youth. It can be observed that the novel is a wonderful work for the use of humor and satire in which he has used various social issues related to Indian society covering broad area of love, marriage, generation gap, dowry, etc. and intends to provide solutions. Among the contemporary writers Bhagat emerges as a realistic writer with objective opinion but leaves his readers to consider the prospective solutions of the problems they are grappling with.

Chetan Bhagat is a writer of modern India who tries hard to put many problems of youth through his novels. He is the symbol of new India and truly called the torch bearer of the unafraid generation. All his novels are touched with the objection to the deep concern of Indian youth, the problems, hopes and aspirations of the younger generation of the society. His area of concern is the length and breadth of the entire country especially of the urban youth. He uses different techniques using humour and satire to hit at these problems. Bhagat's major concern is to remove the conservative attitude and the false myths of our society. The novel *Half Girlfriend* contains a harsh criticism on the true picture of Indian society in contemporary times. He comments on the problems faced by the Indian youth to fulfill their aspirations and the faulty education system of the nation. Bhagat's sixth novel *Half Girlfriend* (2014) portrays the young adult romance in a comic way that attracts huge number of readers. The novel starts with interaction with Chetan Bhagat and Madhav Jha, a Bihari boy in a hotel. The course of interaction compelled the writer to convert it to a novel, named as *Half Girlfriend.* The title itself is funny and eye catching. It is a charming love story. The novel holds the attention of the readers because of its funny elements. Bhagat always takes up the issues which resonate with the masses. He touches on the problem of rural educational system of India. His writing style appears to be like simplistic literature of Earnest Hemingway and R.K.Narayan. He has his own style of writing simple, relatable and entertaining lovely stories. This novel is light hearted and full of fun with a criticism to social problems. The strange title itself is humorous and allures the attention of the readers at first sight. It will make you laugh many times. In Indian society normally boys and girls are not clear about their relationship status with each other. On the other hand, an Indian youth may have wrong notions about girls. Most of the times he thinks that he is more than a friend with a girl, but the girl is still not his girlfriend. Hence, a humorous title is assigned to the topic '*Half Girlfriend.*" The novelist very often tries to create laughter among the readers throughout the story. Throughout the novel Bhagat has been successful in using tremendous skill of humor and satire and beautifully presents a common tale of common man of India. The novel is entertaining. Bhagat ensures reader's engagement for the most part of the book and there is simple humor peppered throughout the story with ample entertainment and that holds mass appeals. After all it's a charming love story that provides a lot of humor and satire to the readers. Indian English has gone through a lot of changes from its inception to the present time on the basis of attainment of a new intensity in terms of concept and presentation. All the three novelists are ease with the language and use an approach to reach at the readers. All of them got immense popularity through their techniques of using humor and satire in their works.

The ongoing debate on Bhagat needs some clarity. We can't question whether he is a literary figure or not. Keeping in view his books and their contents, we can easily observe the elements of literature., i.e., fictive background, ironical temper; imaginative impulse, comical vein, reformatory zeal, etc. that largely constitute the corpus of any literary piece. From all these angles, he stands as a literary figure.

Bibliography

Abrams, Meyer Howard, and Geffrey Harpham. *A Glossary of Literary Terms*. Cengage Learning, 2011. Print.

Adam, Ian. and Helen Tiffin. *Past the Last Post-colonialism and Post-modernism*, New York: Prentice Hall/ Harvester Wheatsheaf, 1991. Print.

Akash Kapoor, "*Up in Smoke*", Sunday Book Review, The New York Times, Jul 2, 2006.

Albert, Edward. *History of English Literature*, Oxford University Press, New Delhi, 1979.

Anjana Sharma, *The Hindu*, January 21, 2001.

Ascroft, Bill., *Garreth Griffiths, and Helen Tiffin*. The Postcolonial Studies: The Key Concepts. New York: Routledge, 2009. Print.

Bhagat, Chetan. *Half Girlfriend*, Rupa & Co, New Delhi, 2014.

.... *2 States-the Story of My Marriage*. Rupa & Co, New Delhi, 2009.Print.

.... *Five Point Someone*. New Delhi: Rupa &Co.2009.

.... *The 3 Mistakes of My Life*. New Delhi: Rupa Publications India Pvt.Ltd.2008.

Bhattacharya, Soumya. "*The Mammaries o the Welfare State* by Upamanyu Chatterjee." *The Hindustan Times*. www.complete review.com Accessed 20 Jul 2016.

Chatterjee, Upamanyu. *English August*: An Indian Story. London: Fber & Faber, 1988. Print.

.... *Way .to Go*. Penguin Books India Ltd. 2010. Print.

.... *Weight Loss*. Penguin Books India Ltd. 2006. Print.

.... *Mammaries of the Welfare State*. Penguin Random House India Pvt. Ltd. Gurgaon: 2001. Print.

Chesterton, G.K. *The Spice of Life and othere Essays*. Beaconsfield: Darwen Finlayson, 1964.

Dahiya, Bhim. S. *A New History of English Literature*. Delhi: Doaba Publications, 2010. Print.

Daiches, David. *A Critical History of English Literature*. Vol. II: The Restoration to the Presentday. New Delhi: Supernova Publishers and Distributers Pvt Ltd. 2014. Print.

Danziger, P. *The Cat Ate my Gymsuit*, New York: Dell. 1974.

Datta, Ketaki. *Indo Anglian Literature*: Past to Present. Kolkatta: Books Way. 2008.print.

Doctor, Geeta. Rev. of *English August: An Indian Story*. Literature Alive. Vol.3 No.2 Dec. 1989. Print.

Evans, Ifor. *A Short History of English Literature*. LondonAELBS, 1963.

Fletcher, M.D. *Contemporary Political Satire: Narrative Strategies in the Post-Modern Context*. M aryland: Lanham, 1987.

Hague, Angela. Irish Murdoh's *Comic Vision. Selinsgrove: Susquehanna* UP. 1984. Print.

Hillenbrand, Margaret. *Literature, Modernity, and the Practice of Resistance: Japanese and Tainese Fiction,* Leiden: Brill, 2007.

Iyengar, K.R.S. *Indian writing in English,* New Delhi, Sterling Publication, 2003, Print.

Keenoy.K.C. *The Nature of Humour*, in the Irish Monthly72 (849) pp.112-119

Khair, Tabish. Ed. *Amitav Ghosh: A Critical Companion*. New Delhi: Permanent Black, 2013. Print.

Mathur, Anurag. *Making the Minister Smile*. New Delhi: Penguin Books India, 2002.Print.

.... *The Country is Going To The Dogs*. New Delhi: Rupa Publications India Pvt. Ltd.2014.Print.

.... *The Department of Denials*. New Delhi, Penguin Books India Pvt. Ltd.2004.

.... *The Inscrutable Americans*. New Delhi: Rupa Publications India Pvt. Ltd.2011.Print.

Keenoy. K. C. *The Nature of Humour* in the Irish Monthly p.112

Michael, Larry J. *The Medicine of laughter: Spurgeon's Humour*, 2003.London: Passmore and Albaster,

Matz, Jesse. *The Modern Novel: A short Introduction.* New Delhi: Atlantic Publishers & Distributers Pvt. Ltd, 2004. Print.

Mehrotra, Arvind Krishna. *A Concise History of Indian Literature in English.* New Delhi: Permanent Black. 2008.

Mengham, Rod. *An Introduction to Contemporary Fiction.* Cambridge: Polity Press, 1999.Print.

Meredith, George. And Maura C. Ives. *George Meredith's Essay on Comedy and Other New Quartely Magazine Publications: A Critical Edition.* Lewisburg: Bucknell UP, 1988. Print.

Mukharjee, Meenakshi. *Realism and Reality: The Novel and Society in India.* Oxford University Press, 1985. Print.

Murphy, Rex. "*Satire Has Forgotten Its Function.*" *The Globe and Mail*, 2006. Vol. A.

Naik, M.K. and Shyamala. A. Narayan. *Indian English Literature 1980-2000: A Critical Survey.* New Delhi: Pencraft, 2001. Print.

Naik, M.K. *Dimensions of Indian English Literature*, New Delhi: Sterling Publishers, 1985.Print.

Naik, M.K.ed. *Aspects of Indian Writing in English. N*ew Delhi: Macmillan, 1999. Print

Naik, M.K. *A History of Indian English Literature.* New Delhi: Sahitya Academy, 1982.

Naik.M.K. *A History of Indian English Literature*, D.G. Offset, Kolkata, 2010

Naikar, Basavaraj. *Indian English Literature.*Vol.1, New Delhi: Atlantic Publishers and Distributors, 2002.

Nema, Nidhi. "Upamanyu Chatterjee Deconstructed." *Research Journal of English Language and Literature* (RJEAL), Vol.4, Issue-2.2016.

Palmer, Jerry. *Taking Humour Seriously.* London: Routledge. 1994.Print.

Palmeri, Frank. *Satire in Narrative.* Austin: University of Texas Press, 1990.

Paranjape, Makarand. R. Making India: *Colonialism, National Culture and Indian English Literature.* New Delhi: 2015.Print.

Patnaik, Jitendra Narayan, *Post Modern Indian English Fiction*, Adhayan Publishers & Distributors, New Delhi, 2012. Print.

Rao, Urmila. *One Swallow for a Summer,* The Hindu, 5 Jan 2010. www. The hindu.com. Accessed 15 Jan 2017.

Ross, Alison. *The Language of Humour.* London: Routledge. 1998. Print.

Sandhu, Nirmal. "The Mammaries o the Welfare State by Upamanyu Chatterjee." 7 Jan 2001, *The Sunday Tribunes,* www.complete-review.com.Accessed 21 Jul 2016.

Scott, F.A. *A concise Dictionary of Current Literary Terms.* London: Macmillan Press Ltd, 1965.

Sharma, Anjana. "*The Mammaries of the Welfare State* by Upamanyu Chatterjee." *The Hindu,* 21 Jan 2001,www.complete-review.Accessed 20 Jul 2o15.

Singh, Anita. *Indian English Novel in the Nineties and after. A Study of the Texts and its Context.* New Delhi: Adhyan Publishers and Distributers, 2004.

Singh, R. P. *The Concept of Anti-Hero in the Novels of Upamanyu Chatterjee.* Bareilly: Prakash Book Depot, 2010. Print.

Singh, R.P. "The Mammaries of the Wefare State: 'Every Day of Moral Degradation'" *The Quest* 16.2: December 2002. 50-52

Singh, R.S. *Indian Novel in English. New Delhi: Arnold-Heinemann.* 1977. Print.

Singh, R.S. *Indian Novel in English: A Critical Study.* New Delhi: Heinneman, 1977. Print

Srivastava, Ramesh K. Wit and Humour in Indian English Literature. Jalandhar: ABS Publications, 2008. Print.

Tharoor, Shashi, *The Great Indian Novel,* New Delhi, Penguin, 1989, Print.

The Oxford Companion to English Literature, ed.by. Margaret Drable, Oxford, Oxford University Press, 1985, p.867.

The Oxord English Dictionary, Vol XI, 1989, P.500.

Tilak, Raghukul. History of English Literature with Social Background Chaucer to Present day. Surjeet Publications, Delhi: 2014.

Thrall, William, Addition Hibbard, and C. Hugh Holman, eds., *A Handbook to Literature.* New York: Odessy Press.1960.

Tiffin, Helen. "Post-Coloninilism, Post-Modernism and the Rehabilitation of Post-Colonial History," *Journal of Common wealth Literature,* 23:1(1988)

Tilak, Raghukul. *History of English Literature with Social Background Chaucer to Present day*. Delhi: Surjeet Publication. Print.

Twain, Mark. *Adventures of Huckleberry Finn*. New York: Dover, 1994.Print.

Web Source

Murphy, Rex. "Satire Has Forgotten Its Function." *The Globe and Mail*, 2006. Vol. A.Sep.09. 2006.https://www.theglobalmail.com>news. Accessed 16 March 2016

www.tor.com >2010/09/16 >interview…Accessed 12 Apr. 2016

https://es.scribd.com >presentation >humour. Accessed 23 Apr. 2016

Akram, Mahammad. "A Short Summary the Ideas of the Welfare State in Upamanyu Chatterjee's Fiction". Rev. *An International Journal of Multidisciplinary Research.* ISN: 2348-2052, Vol. 1, Issue 5, May 2014. Accessed 12 May 2016.

Dirda, Michael. "Review", Wasington Post. 23 April 2006, www.wasingtonpost.com >2006/04/20. Accessed 21 Apr 2016.

Nidhi, Nema. Rev. "Exploration of Latent Irony in Explicit Grotesquery of Upamanyu Chatterjee's Weight Loss." Vol. 3. Issue. 2, 2016 *International Journal of English Language, Literature and Transition Studies,* ISSN2349-9451(0nline), www.rjelal.com >80-85 Dr. Nidh…Accessed 11 Jan 2016.

Raju. M. David. Book Rev. "Black Humour and Ennui in Upamanyu Chatterjee's English August: An Indian Story." *The Criterion,* Dec 13 Vol. 4 Issue- VI.

Rao, Urmila. "One Swallow for a Summer," *The Hindu,* 5 Jan 2010.www.thehindu.com.Accessed 15 Jan 2017.

Mukhija, Nikhil. *The Inscrutable Americans by Anurag Mathur,* Dec 31, 2011.betweenthelines.in > 2011/2012 > book-review-the-inscrutable-amer...Accessed 11 May 2016

www.economictimes.indiatimes.com>news,Accessed 17 Apr 2017

https://books.google.co.in,Accessed 17 April 2017

https://en.m.wikipedia.org>wiki>Anur...Accessed 18 Apr 2017

https://www.goodreads.com. Accessed 18 Apr 2017

www.tcsion.com>oxford>archives>m... Accessed 20 Apr 2017

www.goodreads.com /book/show/22874559-half-girlfriend, Accessed 25th Nov. 2016.

www.sarthakahuja. com/2014/11/summary-review-of-half - girlfriend-chetan-bhagat.html. Accessed 14 Nov. 2016.

www. timesofindia.indiatimes.com>chetan. Accessed 23 Nov. 2016.

www.decanchronicle.com>chetan bhagat, Accessed 26. Nov 2016.

https://literary devices.net, Accessed 10 Jan. 2017.

https://en.m.wikipedia.org.Accessed 18 Apr. 2017

Index

A

Administrative functionaries, 51
Anti-colonial assertion, 39

B

Backward Bihar, 87
Bhagat, Chetan, 9, 11, 12, 14, 16, 18, 20, 29, 36, 37, 41, 42, 55, 83, 87, 88, 89, 90, 97, 98, 99, 100, 102, 112, 113, 116, 117, 118, 119, 120
Black humor, 60
Bureaucratic conditions, 48

C

Central Sahitya Academy award, 41, 43
Civil servants function, 15, 44
Commercial purpose, 66
Constructive social criticism, 13
Contemporary novelists., 12
Contemporary writers, 14, 19, 36, 111, 119
Creative literary works, 42
Cultural communities, 100, 118

D

Dysfunctional bureaucrats, 21

E

East India Company, 108
Eighteenth-century England, 24
Emotional embarrassment, 27
English Romantics, 24
English-speaking monsters, 90

F

Fictional account, 16
Fictional narratives, 11, 20, 36, 40, 86

G

Gandhian Movements, 25
Government accountant, 81
Gradual democratization, 24

H

Human follies, 56
Humor literature, 12, 72

I

Idealistic notions., 18
Ill-conceived socialism, 56
Indian English literature, 11, 19, 23, 26, 27, 28, 29, 33, 86, 88, 99, 109
Indian English Novel, 12, 125
Indian post-colonial literature, 17
Indian reading habits, 29
Individualism, 110
Intellectual journey, 38
Intelligent legislation, 49
Internal colonization, 52
International Civil Servant, 39
Irony focuses, 20

L

Lethargic bureaucrats, 54
Literary phenomenon, 24

M

Mammoth apparatus, 15, 115
Matriarchal system, 105
Middle-class Punjabi family, 116

N

Neo-colonial attitude, 12, 34, 36, 113
New York City, 74

P

Poetic pimp, 83
Post-colonial Indian English Literature, 37
Power-hungry politicians, 12, 18, 86, 113
Present-day writing, 16
Psychological forces, 23

R

Red-haired man, 76
Religious controversial writer, 29
Restoration Congreve, 32, 42
Ruthless colonization, 24

S

Sardonic sense, 18, 70, 86
Satiric elements, 18, 19, 42, 115
Satiric way, 30, 83, 87, 108
Self-chosen life style, 106
Self-seeking mindset, 12, 14, 34, 36, 40, 113
Social realism, 26, 27, 28, 37, 114
Socio-economic conditions, 52, 61
Socio-political protest, 32

T

Telegraph comments, 35
Thackeray, William Makepeace, 32
Topical issues, 11, 22, 108, 112
Traditional beliefs, 11, 14, 16, 34, 40, 113

V

Various literary works, 13
Victorian literature, 32
Vigorous individualized portraits, 30

W

Welfare state, 41, 44, 45, 51, 53, 54
Western binary construction, 37
Western philosophy, 111